THE BECOMING OF GOD

An outline of the development of Man's conception of Cosmic Process

Das Werdende, das ewig wirkt und lebt,
Umfass' euch mit der Liebe holden Schranken,
Und was in schwankender Erscheinung schwebt,
Befestiget mit dauernden Gedanken.
(Goethe: *Faust*. Prolog im Himmel).

Evolution, from cosmic star-dust to human society, is a comprehensive and continuous process. It transforms the world-stuff, if I may use a term which includes the potentialities of mind as well as those of matter. It is creative, in the sense that during the process new and more complex levels of organisation are progressively attained; and new possibilities are thus opened up to the universal world-stuff.
Sir Julian Huxley. *Romanes Lecture*, 1943.

By the same author:
Swinburne, a Nineteenth Century Hellene
Thomas Hardy, A Study of his Writings
and their Background

THE
BECOMING OF GOD

*An outline of the development of Man's
conception of Cosmic Process*

By

WILLIAM R. RUTLAND
B.Litt., D.Phil. (Oxon).

SHAKESPEARE HEAD PRESS
OXFORD
1971

© W. R. Rutland 1971

0 631 13790 4

Library of Congress Catalogue
Card No. 70-149152

PRINTED IN GREAT BRITAIN
BY A. T. BROOME AND SON, 18 ST. CLEMENT'S, OXFORD
AND BOUND BY THE KEMP HALL BINDERY, OXFORD

CONTENTS

ACKNOWLEDGEMENTS vi

INTRODUCTION vii

FOREWORD xv

CHAPTER ONE
Nature, God and Process 1

CHAPTER TWO
The Theory of Evolution in English Poetry 27

CHAPTER THREE
The 'Religions of Humanity' 55

CHAPTER FOUR
'Alpha and Omega'. The Vision of Pierre
Teilhard de Chardin 91

EPILOGUE 108

BIBLIOGRAPHY 119

INDEX 121

ACKNOWLEDGEMENTS

Thanks are due to the following for permission to reproduce copyright material: to Collins Publishers for Teilhard de Chardin, *The Phenomenon of Man;* to A. D. Peters and Company for Julian Huxley, *Essays of a Humanist.*

For help with their particular expertise in each case, I am deeply grateful to Pat Beaumont, my son Francis, and Karin Yule. My friendship with the third of them, which resulted from the writing of this book, is to me its greatest reward.

July, 1971

INTRODUCTION

Since this book was written, Man has done something which looks to us now like the most remarkable achievement in the whole history of intelligence on this planet (of which only the last tiny part in time—a few thousand years—is known to us in any detail). He has landed on the Moon. Oceans of ink have been, and will be, spilled on this event. The most suggestive comment that I myself read was a question in the *Economist*, somewhat as follows (I quote from memory): 'Is this a decisive step up another rung of the evolutionary ladder? Are we witnessing something as momentous as the attempt (which there was then no terrestrial intelligence to witness) by aquatic life to exist on land?' No one with any imagination who heard it will, I think, forget the comment of the American astronaut upon what he saw. He quoted the beginning of Genesis: 'In the beginning God created the heaven and the earth. And the earth was without form, and void; and darkness was upon the face of the deep. And the Spirit of God moved upon the face of the waters. And God said, Let there be light: and there was light.' I have heard this acclaimed from the pulpit as a smack in the eye for the 'humanist atheists'. I have also heard it denounced as the incredible manifestation of fundamentalist obscurantism by a technologist who understood nothing but technology. To me it was neither. I saw in it quite simply a most moving expression of Man's awe and veneration in face of the overwhelming beauty and order of the Universe. A contemporary Russian would not have used the word God. An American, brought up in a tradition much older than Christianity, did. Neither of them probably knew any Greek. Both of them would have said, in their own way, 'This is not Chaos. It is Cosmos.'

Since the last world war, and particularly during the last decade or so, some curious things seem to have been happening to human ideas about God. We have been told, largely from the United States, of the 'death of God'. In England, we have had *Honest to God, Exploration into God*, and accounts of *The God I Want*. A reader of the pages which follow, if my title has led him to expect anything of that nature, will be disappointed. These matters are, indeed, discussed in their proper place. But my real purpose has been a different one. I have gone back, not over thirty years, but over more than three hundred. In that period, western man's entire conception of the nature of the Universe in which he finds himself has been fundamentally modified. Not only have his ideas of the scale of Time and Space been enlarged beyond the imagination of the seventeenth century, which considered a physically static world to have been brought into existence, by a Being outside itself, some five thousand years previously, and likely to be brought to an end in a matter of a few centuries. An even more profound change has taken place in human conceptions of the 'natural' and the 'supernatural'; there has grown up an increasing awareness that not only human life, but also everything that surrounds us on this planet, and indeed the whole Universe of which our planet is a part, is subject to mutation. At the deepest level of all, some human minds, at least, have had an intuition that, in the Cosmic Process which is manifestly taking place throughout the whole Universe, there is to be found an indication of the nature of the Ultimate Reality, of which the Universe is a manifestation. That is the best explanation which I can here give of the title of my book.

This title has intrigued, not to say puzzled, many who have heard it. 'Whatever can it mean? Surely you either believe that God exists, or else that He does not. How can He "become", as your title suggests?' To which the answer—at one level—is quite simple. The book, except for a final few pages of Epilogue, is in no sense a statement of my personal religious belief. Still less is it what many unthinking people ask for nowadays: 'A statement of the facts' (one hesitates whether to envy or pity such people). Whether the 'facts' concerning Ultimate Reality will ever become accessible to the intelligence of Homo Sapiens in anything like his present state is—to say the least—doubtful. What is beyond dispute is that, as his knowledge of his environment and (almost entirely within the present century) of his own nature and history, has increased, so have his conceptions of the real nature of the Universe in which he finds himself changed and developed. This book is a very imperfect and partial exposition of the latest of them.

It is my attempt to write an outline chapter in the history of an idea; to me, one of the most fascinating, and for humanity perhaps the most momentous, of all ideas: that the meaning and nature of the Universe now appear to the human intelligence as a Process. I am speaking, of course, only of western man; for of the other branches of humanity I have no knowledge. This idea, that the Ultimate Reality is, or at least appears to us to be, a process, is, as I have said, comparatively young in the history of human thought. It is hardly older than the early seventeenth century; and is contemporary with the beginnings of science, in the modern sense of that word. I am, of course, well aware that it was the release, at the Renaissance, of the human intellect from earlier, unscientific, modes of thought, which made such a beginning possible.

The first major reorganisation of thought was the entire recasting of the cosmological conception that our planet lay at the centre of the Universe. This was achieved by Copernicus and Galileo; and with them my book begins. That part of the story is familiar to any educated reader. I have tried to tell the story from there. It would have little interest or meaning unless it started at the beginning, though the beginning is now so familiar, and therefore uninteresting. The interest should grow as the plot develops. The latest developments bring us to our own day. It is because I do not know of any account of this development, considered as a continuous, and *still continuing*, development, of the human conception of Cosmic Process, that I have tried to give one.[1]

The reader must not look in these pages for the usual analysis of the results of exhaustive research. What I have attempted is a synthesis. I have tried to show the growth of the idea of Cosmic Process by a few, very carefully chosen, illustrative examples. Some of these may at first seem surprising in such a context, e.g. the passages from Rousseau and Wordsworth. We are familiar

---

[1] There are innumerable books upon various aspects of it. Of the far fewer studies that consider it as a whole, the following are perhaps the most noteworthy (all of them written from a markedly philosophical angle): Samuel Alexander: *Space, Time and Deity* (1916); Conwy Lloyd Morgan: *Emergent Evolution* (1923) and *Life, Mind and Spirit* (1926); A. N. Whitehead: *Process and Reality* (1929). Although only the first instalment of what might have been a magnum opus, Jan Smuts: *Holism* (1928) expounds a suggestive hypothesis about the *modus operandi* of Cosmic Process. The anthropological and sociological aspects are interestingly discussed in the writings of Gerald Heard, e.g. *The Ascent of Humanity* (1929), *The Emergence of Man* (1931) and *Pain, Sex and Time* (1939). His is a popular rather than a scientific approach, but provides evidence of widespread interest in the whole subject.

with them in connection with the Romantic movement in literature. They are in fact illustrations of the whole 'climate of opinion' of the later eighteenth century, as I hope the use which I have made of them will show. My problem has been one of exclusion rather than comprehensiveness. To cast my net wider has been a constant temptation; the book could easily have been three times as long. Perhaps it ought to have been; but there was a very great danger of its getting out of hand. Deliberately, therefore, I have picked and chosen very drastically in order to make a coherent and convincing case, from an enormous mass of evidence which, had I adopted current techniques, would have been set out *in extenso*.

But to do this would require a lifetime. It would fill a hundred volumes; and it would be unreadable. Moreover, to do it properly would, for one man, be impossible; for it would demand mental equipment which no one man possesses, or, in our day, could possibly possess. I commend this point to the contemporary would-be reformers who advocate the 'widening' of our English education. If they do me the honour of reading my book, they will have evidence of the results of a 'specialised' English education which began nearly sixty years ago. If they themselves, presumably with the advantages of a much 'wider' education, will write a better book on the subject to show how it should be done, we shall have a convincing demonstration of the soundness of their case.

The method which I adopted involved selection, and the selection obviously depended upon what I knew to be my interests, and thought to be my knowledge. My interests lie primarily in literature, especially poetry, and in the history of ideas as these make their appearance in creative literature. While some knowledge of Philosophy, and some command of philosophical expertise, are obviously involved, formal philosophy does not in fact make very much appearance. The professional philosophers have, broadly speaking, confined themselves to an entirely abstract world. Of Spinoza it has, indeed, been necessary to speak. But we learn hardly anything of man's conception of Cosmic Process from any other major philosopher of modern times; far less, for example, from Kant and Hegel than from Goethe and Tennyson. The poets were deeply interested in what science was discovering about the physical Universe; its implications were of the greatest significance to them. But the philosophers were almost wholly concerned with the purely metaphysical excogitations of their own minds.

The same considerations apply, in part, to the theologians. In a book with such a title, it would at first sight seem that theology must occupy a considerable place. But the world of the theologian, like that of the philosopher, tends largely to be a closed one, inhabited by himself and his fellow theologians. Their primary concern should not be at all with the world of physical phenomena. We all know, as a matter of history, that the theologians embarked upon a misguided crusade, out of their proper sphere into the sphere of physical phenomena; with results ultimately most damaging to theology. In the seventeenth century they made Galileo, who had demonstrated that it did, say that the Earth did NOT revolve around the Sun. In the nineteenth, one of them cried from the pulpit of the University Church of St. Mary the Virgin in Oxford: 'Leave me my ancestors in Paradise and I will leave you yours in the zoological gardens!' But with the conflict between Religion and Science I have not much been concerned here. That story has been told many times.

I have myself told it, as it concerned the development of Thomas Hardy.[1] It is only when we come to our own day that certain recent developments in theology have had to be taken into account. As will be seen, the boot is now upon the other foot. The objective of the theologians whose names appear in these pages has been to adapt their theology to the lay mind of contemporary man.

I have said that my selection of material to illustrate the emergence of Man's conception of Cosmic Process, has—inevitably—been made in accordance with my own preferences in literature, and my own knowledge. I know of no writer, whether in the field of creative imagination or any other, who can compare in this respect with Goethe, for the period of about 1770–1830. Accordingly, it is above all from the writings of Goethe that my illustrations are taken for the first chapter, 'Nature, God and Process'.[2] Similarly, when it comes to illustrating the impact of

---

[1] Ch. 3 of my *Thomas Hardy: a Study of his Writings and their Background*. New York (Russell and Russell) 1962; original edn. Basil Blackwell, Oxford, 1938.

[2] Of every German quotation given in the text, I have provided an English translation. These claim nothing beyond giving the basic 'prose' sense to anyone who does not read German fluently. No translation of poetry can ever give more

evolutionary ideas in the first three quarters of the nineteenth century, there is no writer in Western European literature known to me who illustrates it so well as Tennyson.[1] My second chapter is devoted largely to him. My third chapter deals with the creations of the lay mind of modern man; which were, of course, part of the same tide of human thought. I have called this chapter 'The "Religions of Humanity" '; using the phrase in the sense in which it was first used by the founder of the original one. This particular phase of Man's thinking really began with the French Revolution; which marked the end of Christendom as it had existed—the Reformation notwithstanding—at least since the days of Charlemagne. In one important sense, the Protestantism resulting from the Reformation, and notably the Anglican church (which is certainly a 'reformed' church, whether or not it may correctly be called 'protestant'), was itself part of Christendom. It shared the basic theological assumptions concerning God with the Church of Rome. But the Religion of Humanity discarded the theological Divinity altogether. As may be seen in the concluding pages of my third chapter, the contemporary versions of it continue to do so.

My last chapter is concerned with one of the most remarkable writers of the twentieth century. Père Teilhard de Chardin's *Le Phénomène humain* is still the subject of acute controversy. Perhaps the most remarkable aspect of it is that it attempts, in some sort, a synthesis of the fundamental doctrine of the Roman church, of which Teilhard was a priest, with a sort of Religion of Humanity.

---

than part of the original, sometimes the least significant part; this is particularly true of a poet so profound, so condensed and so permeated with the genius of the German language—of which he is probably the supreme exemplar—as Goethe. For invaluable help with many of them, I am greatly indebted to the scholarship and kindly co-operation of Miss Karin Yule.

Quotations from *Faust* presented a problem of their own. *Faust* is probably the most untranslatable of all the great masterpieces of modern literature. I consulted every standard, and at least one contemporary, translation; intending to use versions from them which would at least not be bald prose. It proved, however, that if my reader were not to lose something *essential* to the sense of the original, only prose could fulfil the requirement. As an example, I mention the song of the *Erdgeist*. Even Carlyle's version of this leaves out certain things in the original, to understand which is indispensable to proper comprehension of the passage.

[1] The substance of my second chapter was originally published as a paper, entitled 'Tennyson and the Theory of Evolution', in *Essays and Studies* by members of the English Association, vol. XXVI (Clarendon Press, 1940). This has been quoted and referred to many times (e.g. in *Evolution and Poetic Belief*, by G. Roppen, Oslo University Press, 1956). But it has never been contradicted, corrected or added to; from which I assume that scholars have accepted it. It has never been reprinted or published in book form.

He attempts, not only to place Humanity within the Cosmic Evolutionary Process, but also to make Humanity itself the active agent, henceforth, of this process upon our planet. I should add that, as any reader of my fourth chapter will see, I have deliberately confined myself to *Le Phénomène humain*. Not only is that his magnum opus; it is the one among his writings wholly germane to my purpose. Even with that, I have confined myself almost wholly to exposition, and avoided the controversies that are still raging round it. They do not affect its value as evidence of the growth of Man's conception of Cosmic Process.

In conclusion, something should perhaps be said of two (out of many) matters which have been deliberately omitted. I hesitated as to whether to discuss the contributions made to the philosophy of becoming ('la philosophie du devenir') in the early years of this century by Hardy and Bergson; the first with his doctrine of 'The Immanent Will' in *The Dynasts*; the second with his 'élan vital' in *L'Evolution créatrice*.

On consideration, I decided to omit Hardy because I have already said all I have to say on the subject. The book was first published in 1938; but it has been reprinted both in New York and Tokyo, and is readily available.[1] Bergson I have omitted (somewhat to my regret) because to do him justice would demand a separate book. Not even a summary of his philosophy of Creative Evolution could be understood without an exposition of his very difficult theories concerning (i) mind and matter, (ii) intelligence and instinct, (iii) time and duration ('la durée').[2] Expressed in superb French, and with admirable lucidity, Bergson's work has all the panoply of a full-blown metaphysic; but it may well be closer to the realities of the phenomenal universe that we know than that of many of his great predecessors.

In England, metaphysics has—at least for the time being—been silenced by 'linguistic analysis'. Before this took place, A. N. Whitehead published his Gifford Lectures in 1929 in a volume entitled *Process and Reality: an Essay in Cosmology*. This perfectly illustrates the purely philosophical approach to Cosmic Process. A quotation from the final chapter 'God and the World' will

[1] Op. cit.
[2] I am not alone in finding Bergson abstruse and difficult. See Bertrand Russell: *History of Western Philosophy*, p. 820 *et seq.*

illustrate how metaphysical treatment of the theme of the pages that follow differs from that of both creative artists and scientists; it may explain why I have, on the whole, eschewed pure metaphysics:

'God and the World are the contrasted opposites in terms of which Creativity achieves its supreme task of transforming disjointed multiplicity, with its diversities in opposition, into concrescent unity, with its diversities in contrast. In each actuality there are two concrescent poles of realisation—'enjoyment' and 'appetition', that is the physical and the conceptual. For God the conceptual is prior to the physical, for the World the physical poles are prior to the conceptual poles.'

The Epilogue, written as a result of the comments of a reader of the typescript of my book, speaks for itself. Apart from the opening paragraphs (which refer to a point in my final chapter), it stands by itself as an explanation, in purely personal terms, of why the book was written. Any reader who would like to know more of the author than can be learnt from the book itself might well go to it from here, as a second, quite different, Introduction. And if he regrets the absence of Bergson from the main body of my text, he will find him there.

To the Bishop of Salisbury I am deeply grateful for his Foreword, as anyone would be who had such things written about him by such a man, but also because I know what does not publicly appear—how precious was the time he gave up to do it. As he supposed, I knew nothing of Peter Hamilton, who came to Marlborough twenty years after I did, or his book. This I have just read. It is almost entirely a treatise upon the New Theology in relation to process philosophy. My book is almost entirely a history of the emergence, since the seventeenth century, of a consciousness, in creative literature, which has culminated in process philosophy; and it is written by a literary scholar who has no pretensions to being a theologian. There are many different paths towards The Unity; upon which, if they do not lead men astray, all finally converge.

FOREWORD

BY THE BISHOP OF SALISBURY

I have known William Rutland on and off since we were at the same Preparatory School during the first World War. When therefore he asked me to write a Foreword to his book, *The Becoming of God*, I felt I could not refuse. When I came to read his book, I realised to my surprise that this work of a former Head of the Department of Modern Languages at Marlborough College, was on almost the same subject as another book, *The Living God and the Modern World* (Hodder and Stoughton, 1967) by the Rev. Peter Hamilton, a former Chaplain of the same College.

They did not overlap at the College, and as far as I know, neither knew of the other's existence, let alone of his writings. So, as *ex-officio* Chairman of the Marlborough Council, I asked myself whether the appointment as masters there of men of a certain quality of mind and outlook, evident in this striking similarity of subject, might not be connected with something about the character of the College. I found the thought fascinating, and the book, in consequence, especially interesting.

Hamilton comes to the subject from a background of Mathematics and Science; Rutland approaches it from the side of poetry and the arts. Hamilton goes into the questions raised by the so-called New Theology at some depth; Rutland's treatment of it is, as he candidly admits, not that of a professional theologian. While Hamilton's inspiration comes from the work of Alfred North Whitehead, Rutland's is derived from Alfred Lord Tennyson. Each is deeply concerned with Teilhard de Chardin's contribution towards a convergence of the scientific and religious interpretations of the Universe.

What I like about Rutland is his breadth of vision and, even more, his warmth of feeling. He is trying to penetrate behind superficial differences to underlying unities and indeed towards The Unity. He knows that, though theology may sometimes be treated like any other specialised departmental subject, religion can never be. Either it is the way we look at the whole of life, or it is no religion worthy of the name for the twentieth century, or, indeed, for any other.

What I am not sure about is whether *The Becoming of God* is, or could be, balanced by another book on *The Being of God*. I know that those who stress The Becoming argue that becoming includes being, whereas being does not include becoming. Thus, for example, Hamilton makes the point that motion includes rest as a special state, but not the converse. I remain unconvinced. Perhaps in human understanding The Becoming and The Being must stand side by side as much towards the end of the second millenium A.D. as towards the end of the second millenium B.C. This is the exciting possibility that arises from what I believe to be the correct exegesis of the great passage about the revelation of the Divine Name in the third chapter of the Book of Exodus.

The meaning of YHVH is contained neither in our traditional translation, I AM THAT I AM, nor in the revised Version marginal variant, I WILL BE THAT I WILL BE, but in both together. I agree with Martin Buber that behind the definition lies the exclamation, HE!, and I like his rendering *I shall be there as HE who I there shall be* (cf. M. Buber: *Moses*, East and West Library, Oxford and London, 1946, pp. 39 ff.)

Those who interpret God in static propositional terms seem so often to be trying to get Him within their grasp. This whole approach of theology can easily degenerate into the supreme idolatry of lust, unless it is balanced by dynamic conceptions of a Deity who is love, and who is never to be in our grasp, but who longs to have us, together with the entire Universe, in his. Rutland is feeling towards such a conception.

It took Dietrich Bonhoeffer a long time to realise that 'the lure of theology', in Eberhard Bethge's splendid phrase, summing up the first part of his life, is no substitute for the reality of the Christian religion, however 'religionless' that may be. If we are not just to fall into the temptation of identifying theology and religion, we badly need an understanding of reality, a total view of the Universe, in which the emotions and the will are as much involved as the intellect. That is where Rutland is for me important. He makes me feel the warmth of the cosmic process of love, and he makes me want to identify myself with it.

He has his links with Teilhard de Chardin, but they seem to me to be less significant than his links with Tennyson. We do not know the inner agonies of Teilhard's mind and soul, though we can guess them. With Tennyson it is different. He lets us see the inner agonies of his soul. For someone who might be regarded as a quintessential Victorian, this is a staggering self-exposure. If Teilhard attempts a theology of the Universe, Tennyson reveals a religion, grappling in *In Memoriam* with the problem of shattering new knowledge and overwhelming personal sorrow.

I do not agree with all that Rutland says, and some of what he says I cannot understand. But I am told that the Lord my God is one Lord, and I am told to love the Lord my God with all my heart and with all my soul and with all my mind and with all my strength; and, furthermore, I am told I cannot do this on my own—this God is not mine but ours (cf. Deut. 6, 41 and Mark 12, 29f.)

I do not find it at all easy to believe what I am told to believe or to do what I am told to do. I need grace, and I am grateful for any help, any 'means of grace'. It is because *The Becoming of God* has helped me and has been in that sense 'a means of grace' that I regard it as a privilege to be asked to write this foreword and commend it to others.

✠ JOSEPH SARUM.

B

CHAPTER ONE

NATURE, GOD AND PROCESS

The theory of creation familiar to the Western World for more than twenty centuries is to be found in the first and second chapters of *Genesis*. What is for convenience called the Mosaic hypothesis (without, in our time, making any claim for its invention by Moses) contains two fundamental assumptions, the geocentric and the anthropocentric. It assumes that the earth is the centre of the Universe; and that Man, created 'in the image of God', is the original ruler of the Earth, under the Creator (Gen. 1, 28), and from the completion of the creative process, its most important inhabitant. Upon the anthropocentric hypothesis no serious assault was made until the second half of the eighteenth century. The geocentric hypothesis was destroyed by Copernicus in the sixteenth. For the Ptolemaic system, according to which the Earth lay at the centre of the Universe, while the stars revolved about it in concentric spheres, Copernicus and Galileo showed that the Earth revolved round the sun.

The cosmological aspect of the matter, to describe the geocentric hypothesis in different language, is taken in the Bible as a matter of course; and is of quite minor importance compared with the theological aspect, that of the relationship between God and Man. To Copernicus and Galileo, true sons of the Renaissance, the geocentric hypothesis was exclusively a scientific problem like many others, e.g. the oscillations of a pendulum, to be investigated by strictly scientific methods. But the authorities of the Roman Catholic Church held quite different views. It was intolerable that anyone should teach that the Earth revolved round the Sun when the Book of Joshua explicitly states the precise opposite. Copernicus escaped persecution by the circumstance that his book, '*De revolutionibus orbium coelestium*', though finished in 1530, was not published until just before his death in 1543. Galileo, the inventor of the telescope, with which he discovered not only the mountains on the Moon, which so impressed the young Milton, but also four of the satellites of Jupiter, was less fortunate. In 1616 he was cited before the Holy Inquisition to answer for propagating heresy, a doctrine both philosophically (we should say 'scientific-ally') absurd and manifestly contrary to Holy Scripture. At the same time, the book of Copernicus was put on the *Index Librorum Prohibitorum*, on which it remained for a century and a half (until 1757). Galileo, however, apart from being forbidden to continue his teaching, escaped serious consequences until 1632. He was then summoned to Rome by Pope Urban VIII, and made to recant (he was by then an old man) his pernicious heresy. The moons of Jupiter, meanwhile, continued to revolve round the planet, and the planets round the sun. As Galileo is reported to have said after his recantation (unfortunately, the story is almost certainly apocryphal), 'All the same, it *does* move'.[1]

In that same year, 1632, there was born in Holland, whither his family had fled to escape from the Holy Inquisition, a Jew, Spinoza, who has been called 'the noblest and most lovable of the great philosophers'.[2] His greatest work was unpublished when he died, at 43, of tuberculosis, produced by the polishing of lenses, which earned him a living; and for a century thereafter was not widely known. When it was known, it was most violently attacked. As Bertrand Russell says:

> Intellectually, some other (great philosophers) have sur-passed him, but ethically he is supreme. As a natural conse-quence, he was considered during his lifetime and for a century after his death, a man of appalling wickedness. He was born a Jew, but the Jews excommunicated him. Christians abhorred him equally; although his whole philosophy is dominated by the idea of God, the orthodox accused him of atheism. Leibniz, who owed much to him, concealed his debt, and carefully abstained from saying a word in his praise; he even went so far as to lie about the extent of his personal acquaintance with the heretic Jew.[3]

A century after his death, Spinoza's *Ethics* spoke to some of the foremost minds of the later eighteenth century. Both Goethe and Coleridge were students and admirers of them; and were largely instrumental in giving that work the status it has since enjoyed. They were themselves influenced by it; and through Coleridge, the influence extended to Wordsworth.

[1] 'E pur si muove'; v. *Oxford Dictionary of Quotations*.
[2] Bertrand Russell, *History of Western Philosophy*, p. 592.
[3] Bertrand Russell, *History of Western Philosophy*, p. 592.

The enquiries of Spinoza, in the metaphysical part of the *Ethics*, were not directed to the operations of Nature, pronounced by Man to be contrary to the Word of God; rather to the reality of Nature and God, the relationship between them and the resulting knowledge of what is possible to Man.

The conception of God held in the seventeenth century was that He was an omnipotent, self-sufficient, supernatural Being; who, out of nothing, had created the world, sustains its continued existence, and occasionally intervenes in it in miraculous ways. He will outlast it; and may, indeed, bring it to an end. In a sense at least as old as the nineteenth Psalm, His creation reveals of its Creator that 'The heavens declare the glory of God and the firmament showeth His handiwork'; but more intimate revelations of His own moral nature come direct from God Himself.

Spinoza set forth the different view that, instead of Nature, on the one hand, and a supernatural God on the other, there was one single, indivisible world of Reality; this was at once both Nature and God, leaving no room for the 'supranatural'. This view is what is generally called Spinoza's 'pantheism'.[1]

The conception of a supernatural God, just outlined, was almost universal in the seventeenth century. It was held equally by Descartes (1596–1650), the founder of modern philosophy, and by Newton (1642–1727), the founder of Physics as accepted until the early twentieth century.

Spinoza's different conception was essentially a rationalist one. There is, however, a most important distinction to be made between Spinoza and previous thinkers:

> The positive side of rationalism may be seen in the great classics of Science in the sixteenth and seventeenth centuries— the works of Copernicus, Vesalius, Galileo, Gilbert, Kepler, Harvey, Boyle, Descartes, Huygens, Pascal, Leibniz and Newton, to mention only a round dozen of the most famous names of the period. Their discoveries were the positive results of reason, whose main function it is to trace the connection between things, to discover their laws, and to display the order which makes things intelligible. It may be said, without any disrespect for these famous men, that the positive

[1]Although this is one of the senses of the word given in the O.E.D., it is to be distinguished from the more usual connotation of the word; which is the much earlier idea of primitive religion, that everything in Nature possesses its own particular deity.

side of rationalism also found its fullest expression in Spinoza. For he attempted a synthesis of the whole of reality. This attempt shocked some of the above-mentioned geniuses, and would have shocked the rest had they heard of it. For none of them dreamed of the possibility of bridging the chasm between the natural and the supranatural. Spinoza conceived of the whole of reality, including the human and the divine, as an organically interconnected cosmos, in which there is nothing capricious or contingent, but everything happens in an orderly manner according to law.[1]

To seventeenth century conceptions of Nature, the eighteenth century added another, peculiarly its own. This was of enormous importance in literature and the arts generally. It is one of the most typical characteristics of the Romantic Movement—of which it may be said to have been one of the most potent causes; and in its later stages, it produced crucial developments in the history of ideas. Spinoza's conception, objective and rationalist though it was, paradoxically contributed to it (as can be seen in Goethe and Wordsworth). The paradox lies in the fact that this eighteenth century conception of Nature was essentially emotional, subjective and psychological. Put in the simplest possible terms —which are, inevitably, an over-simplification—it amounts to the sentiment, rather than the intellectual concept, a feeling rather than a thought, that Nature is not only a living entity in herself, but also possesses a personality, capable of the emotions of which a human personality is capable; and that between this personality and that of individual human beings there could be established a relationship no less real and vital for being impossible of precise intellectual definition. The thing could be more easily illustrated than described. And the best illustrations are to be found in Wordsworth, much of whose best and most characteristic poetry is full of them. Two will here suffice. The first, a simple one, is from 'Lines written in early Spring':

> The budding twigs spread out their fan,
> To catch the breezy air;
> And I must think, do all I can,
> That there was pleasure there.

This is comparatively simple, though not perhaps quite as simple

[1] Abraham Wolf: article on Spinoza in the *Encyclopedia Britannica*.

The development of a philoso. (Spinoza) and poetic identification (Wordsworth) w/ nature in the 18th century.

NATURE, GOD AND PROCESS 5

as appears at first sight. The second cannot be called simple, by any standards. In 'Tintern Abbey' Wordsworth recollecting his boyhood, thus addresses his sister:

> Oh! yet a little while
> May I behold in thee what I was once,
> My dear, dear Sister! And this prayer I make,
> Knowing that Nature never did betray
> The heart that loved her; 'tis her privilege,
> Through all the years of this our life, to lead
> From joy to joy; for she can so inform
> The mind that is within us, so impress
> With quietness and beauty, and so feed
> With lofty thoughts, that neither evil tongues,
> Rash judgments, nor the sneers of selfish men,
> Nor greetings where no kindness is, nor all
> The dreary intercourse of daily life,
> Shall e'er prevail against us, or disturb
> Our cheerful faith that all which we behold
> Is full of blessings.

To Wordsworth it will be necessary later to return at greater length. Suffice it here to say that such passages could not possibly have been written a century earlier.[1] They illustrate better than pages of discussion what the eighteenth century added to the conception of Nature.

There have been many histories of the Romantic Movement. I know of none which does full justice to this conception;[2] the importance of which extends far beyond what is usually covered by that term, and indeed becomes part of the history of thought. Some brief account of its emergence is a necessary introduction to what follows. In so far as it is possible to determine the beginning of any idea which later becomes a widely diffused 'climate of opinion', the beginning of this must probably be looked for in the cult of 'sensibilité', which became fashionable in France in the eighteenth century. Since, however, it is no part of our purpose

[1] Both first appeared in *Lyrical Ballads*, 1798.

[2] As far as concerns English, an illuminating account of some of the antecedents is to be found in J. W. Beach: *The Concept of Nature in 19th century English Poetry*. (New York; originally published 1936, but since reprinted by Russell and Russell). On the French and German material, however, it is inadequate.

to rewrite the history of the Romantic Movement, the emergence of the conception of Nature as a living Personality will be illustrated by some passages from a single author, Jean Jacques Rousseau. That extraordinary man has probably exerted as profound an influence upon human ideas, in several directions, as any writer who has ever lived.

His novel *Julie, ou la nouvelle Héloïse* (1761), which was read all over Western Europe, antedates Wordsworth by nearly 40 years; and, although less explicit than in Wordsworth, a deep and all pervading sentiment of 'sympathy' between the hero and heroine on the one hand, and Nature, as she appears in the tremendous scenery of the Lake of Geneva on the other, is perhaps the book's most striking characteristic. As Daniel Mornet has well put it:

> 'All the moving passages of the book seem transfigured by a secret association between the soul of the characters and the great soul of Nature'.[1]

In *Emile* (1762), the famous treatise on the education of the child, which got him into such trouble with the authorities of both Switzerland and France, Rousseau assigns a supremely important part to the properly directed contemplation of Nature. Particularly in Book 3, when the instinctive and almost animal life of the small boy is to be developed into deeper perception and sensibility, Rousseau insists that, were he to take for granted in the child his own feelings about Nature, the adult would be quite wrong:

> Plein de l'enthousiasme qu'il éprouve, le maître veut le communiquer à l'enfant: il croit l'émouvoir en le rendant attentif aux sensations dont il est ému lui-même. Pure bêtise! C'est dans le coeur de l'homme qu'est la vie du spectacle de la nature; pour le voir, il faut le sentir. L'enfant aperçoit les objets; mais il ne peut apercevoir les rapports qui les lient, il ne peut entendre la douce harmonie de leur concert. Il faut une expérience qu'il n'a point acquise, il faut des sentiments qu'il n'a point éprouvés, pour sentir l'impression composée qui résulte à la fois de toutes ces sensations.

It is by the interaction of the growing experience and aware-ness of the young soul with the great soul, Nature, that the true

[1] *The European Inheritance*, Oxford 1954; vol. 2, p. 322.

Rousseau as a Romantic —

education of the former is achieved. This process is, of course, the grand subject of Wordsworth's *Prelude*, of which more hereafter. No better example, in brief, of what Rousseau is here describing could be found than in 'Tintern Abbey', notably in the 40 lines or so beginning:

> And so I dare to hope,
> Though changed, no doubt, from what I was when first
> I came among these hills. . . .

That Rousseau should have given such important roles to Nature, both in his novel and in his treatise on education, is not surprising in view of what Nature meant to him himself. The evidence is perhaps most plentiful in the last book he published *Les Rêveries du Promeneur solitaire* (1765), which is full of it. The Fifth 'Promenade', describing the short period which he spent on the Ile de St. Pierre, in the Lake of Bienne, might, were it not written in prose, claim in this respect to be the first Romantic poem in French.[1] The Third 'Promenade' recounts in short how Rousseau himself underwent the experience which is the origin of the famous 'Profession de Foi du Vicaire savoyard' in *Emile*:

> La méditation dans la retraite, l'étude de la nature, la contemplation de l'univers, forcent un solitaire à s'élancer incessamment vers l'auteur des choses et à chercher avec une douce inquiétude la fin de tout ce qu'il voit et la cause de tout ce qu'il sent.

The Seventh contains a moving description of how the persecution of men drove him for comfort into the arms of Nature:

> Je sens des extases, des ravissements inexprimables à me fondre pour ainsi dire dans le système des êtres, de m'identifier avec la nature entière. Tant que les hommes furent mes frères, je me faisais des projets de félicité terrestre; ces projets étant toujours rélatifs au tout, je ne pouvais être heureux que de la félicité publique, et jamais l'idée d'un bonheur particulier n'a touché mon coeur que quand j'ai vu mes frères ne chercher le

---

[1] One of the first examples of the word itself thus used—which has an interesting history in French—is precisely here: 'Les rives du Lac de Bienne sont plus sauvages et romantiques que celles du Lac de Genève'.

leur que dans ma misère. Alors pour ne pas les haïr, il a bien fallu les fuire; alors, me réfugiant chez la mère commune, j'ai cherché dans ses bras à me soustraire aux atteintes de ses enfants. . . .[1]

In all these passages, and many others, Nature, however imprecise may be the formulation, is given the attributes of a living personality. More than this; considering his attitude as a whole, and various references to God notwithstanding, it can hardly be denied that Rousseau, in the 1760s, used the word Nature for the One Living Reality; for what Wordsworth, nearly half a century later, called

> the one interior Life
> That lives in all things.

The clearest evidence is the following passage from the *Confessions*:[2]

Bientôt de la surface de la terre j'élevais mes idées à tous les êtres de la nature, au système universel des choses, à l'être incompréhensible qui embrasse tout. Alors, l'esprit perdu dans cette immensité, je ne pensais pas, je ne raisonnais pas, je me sentais, avec une sorte de volupté, accablé du poids de cet univers. . . . Je crois que, si j'eusse dévoilé tous les mystères de la nature, je me serais senti dans une situation moins délicieuse que cette étourdissante extase à laquelle mon esprit se livrait sans retenue, et qui, dans l'agitation de mes transports, me faisait écrire quelquefois: 'O grand Etre! O grand Etre!' sans pouvoir dire ni penser rien de plus.

It is impossible to read such passages without being reminded of a conception which, though originally very much older, had to some extent returned to favour in the later eighteenth century. This is the conception of a 'world-soul'. The history of this idea is one of the obscure and difficult by-ways of philosophy; and is to our purpose chiefly because it interested Goethe. It probably goes back originally to Plotinus; it certainly appears in several writers from the Renaissance onwards. Paracelsus (1493–1541) speaks of the 'archeus terrae'; and Giordano Bruno of the 'anima

---

[1] This reference to 'la mère commune' became classic. In the magnificent passage in 'La Maison du Berger' devoted to a refutation of the Romantic view of Nature, Alfred de Vigny makes her say: 'On me dit une mère, et je suis une tombe.'

[2] Published 1781–8. This passage is from the letter to Malesherbes of 26th January, 1762.

Move, Glanvil, Schelling, Pico della Mirandello

terrae'.[1] Two of the Cambridge Platonists, Henry More (1614–87) and Joseph Glanvill (1636–80) carried the idea of an 'anima mundi' into the second half of the seventeenth century.[2] Schelling, at the end of the eighteenth century, wrote *Die Weltseele*, of which more hereafter. Paracelsus and Pico della Mirandola (1463–94), to mention no others, had also spoken of the universe as the 'Macrocosm', the Great Order, and of Man as the 'Microcosm' (i.e. a corresponding Order on a small scale). And here we are brought face to face with Goethe. That Goethe had some knowledge of Plotinus is proved by the fact that the first line of one of his later philosophical poems is a literal translation of one of the most characteristic statements of Plotinus.[3] Goethe is not only, by universal consent, the greatest writer in the German language, and one of the greatest writers of the modern world; he also probably shares with Leonardo da Vinci the distinction of being the nearest approach to a universal genius that humanity has produced.

Born in 1749, he had, by the end of his twenty-sixth year, written most of his masterpiece now known as the First Part of *Faust*. None of it was publicly known until 1790, when there appeared 'Faust: ein Fragment'; although some of his friends, including Schiller, knew, and were intensely interested in, what we now know to have been written fifteen years earlier; and the first edition of the complete First Part appeared in 1808. Everything to be quoted from *Faust*, or referred to, was already written by 1775—unless specifically stated otherwise.[4] The purpose of these quotations is to provide evidence concerning Goethe's conception of Nature and God in the first flush of his manhood and his genius. Without either adding to the huge literature of Faust symbolism, or attributing to Goethe everything that is put into the mouth of his creations, the value of this evidence will

---

[1] Bruno was burnt for heresy in 1600; the date of his birth is uncertain.

[2] Glanvill describes it as 'that of a Mundane Soul, lately revived by that incomparable Platonist and Cartesian, Dr. H. More'; quoted by Basil Willey in *The Seventeenth Century Background*, p. 190.

[3] The poem is 'Vermächtniss', of which the first line is 'Kein Wesen kann zu nichts zerfallen!' The Greek of Plotinus is ἀπόλειται οὐδὲν τῶν ὄντων and W. R. Inge translates: 'nothing that possesses real being can ever perish.' The poem was written in 1829.

[4] We owe it to one of the happiest accidents in literary history that, at the end of 1775 or early in 1776 a certain Fräulein von Göchhausen copied into a commonplace-book what is now called the 'Ur-Faust'. It came to light over a century later, and this 'Göchhausen Transcript' was first published in 1887.

Goethe: Faust

become even more apparent when Goethe's own later utterances are added to it.

At the beginning of the play, Faust is seeking to escape from the stifling confinement of lifeless learning into the 'living Nature into which God created Man':

> Statt der lebendigen Natur,
> Da Gott die Menschen schuf hinein—(414–15)

The 'secret book' of Nostradamus (1503–66, an astrologer, here representing the believers in a world of Spirits) is to help him to this. He lights upon the Sign of the Macrocosm, and at first it seems to reveal to him the secret forces of Nature, and to make him hear the music of the spheres. But he realises that it lacks reality:

> Welch' Schauspiel! aber ach, ein Schauspiel nur!
> Wo fass' ich dich, unendliche Natur?
> Euch Brüste, wo? Ihr Quellen alles Lebens,
> An denen Himmel und Erde hängt,
> Dahin die welke Brust sich drängt—
> Ihr quellt, ihr tränkt, und schmacht' ich so vergebens?[1]

The personification of endless Nature as the Great Mother was nothing very new in 1775; although the conception of her breasts as the sources of all life, upon which Heaven and Earth hang, could hardly have been so expressed before Spinoza's pantheism came to be known.

Faust then reluctantly turns the pages of Nostradamus, and comes upon the Sign of the Spirit of Earth. Here he seems to recognise something akin to himself. He pronounces the secret spell; and in a red flame the Spirit appears (at the first performance in Weimar, Goethe had the Spirit of Earth shown as a gigantic face, rising from mist and filling the whole back of the stage). Though almost overcome with terror ('writhing away like a terrified worm') Faust claims to be his equal. And then the Spirit sings:

[1] What a spectacle! But alas, only a spectacle! Where shall I grasp thee, limitless Nature? Where you, ye breasts? Ye sources of all life, upon which hang heaven and earth, towards which the parched breast presses, ye flow, ye give to drink, and do I languish thus in vain?

In Lebensfluthen, im Thatensturm
Wall' ich auf und ab,
Wehe hin und her!
Geburt und Grab,
Ein ewiges Meer,
Ein wechselnd Weben,
Ein glühend Leben;
So schaff' ich am sausenden Webstuhl der Zeit
Und wirke der Gottheit lebendiges Kleid.[1]

Concerning this, Carlyle asked: 'Of twenty millions that have read and spouted this thunder-speech of the *Erdgeist*, are there yet twenty units of us that have learned the meaning thereof?' (*Sartor Resartus*, ch. 8). The essential meaning is that all life on this planet—and we know no other—is a continuous Process; and that this process is a continuous revelation of indwelling Deity.

For us, in the second half of the twentieth century, it is difficult to realise the revolution in human thought that has taken place since the beginning of the eighteenth. We take it for granted, not only that organic life is a process, but that the same is true of the entire physical universe. There is a current controversy among scientists as to whether the universe had a beginning in time, or is a 'continuous creation'; nobody, however, sufficiently educated to understand the issues supposes it to be static. But what is axiomatic in the nineteen-sixties would have made the sixteen-sixties stare and gasp. More must be said about the scientific aspect of this change when we come to consider the history of the theory of Evolution. Our present concern is with the emergence of the eighteenth century conception of Nature, and what it involved. We have seen how, in the 1760s, Rousseau is apostrophising the 'Great Being'. We see in *Faust* how Goethe, by 1775, not only makes Faust address Nature as 'the source of all life', he also makes the Spirit of Earth the spokesman of a Process which is a revelation of the ultimate Life of the Universe. Wordsworth, as we shall see, felt likewise. By 1798 he described Nature as:

---

[1] 'In floods of life, in the storm of action, I flow up and down, float hither and thither. Birth and the grave, an eternal sea, an ever-changing activity, a glowing life. Thus I fashion upon the humming loom of Time and weave the living garment of Deity'.

> A motion and a spirit, that impels
> All thinking things, all objects of all thought,
> And rolls through all things.

Some such—more or less pantheistic—conception was almost universal by the end of the eighteenth century. But it would be false to suggest that any one conception, capable of precise formulation, dominated the scene. On the contrary, there were a number of ideas which, stated strictly and logically, might seem at variance or even in conflict. But taken together, they did add up to a 'climate of opinion' such as had never before existed. To use an analogy from physics: the light in which Nature and the Universe appeared then, can, indeed, be analysed into a spectrum; whose individual colours may seem very different, but which, taken together, combine into white light.

As an example of one end of the spectrum, a quotation may be given from *The World-Soul*, by the philosopher F. W. J. von Schelling, which first appeared in 1798. Schelling, though of no great importance as a philosopher in his own right, is of historical significance in that, during his early years in Jena, he was not without influence upon the German Romantics, and was a personal friend of Goethe (though he was only half Goethe's age). They shared, for instance, the idea that the physical and the spiritual may be two aspects of one Identity. Goethe was also attracted by Schelling's scientific, rather than metaphysical, approach, which resembled his own, and is well illustrated in Schelling's first considerable book *Ideas for a Philosophy of Nature* (1797). Schelling's position in *The World-Soul* is this: the whole physical cosmos does indeed make up, or contain, a living Entity, or 'world-soul', but the process which is Nature is a closed one, a cycle continuously repeated; and it is the 'organising Principle' causing this cyclic process which is the World-Soul:

> In Nature, everything strives forward continuously; the cause of this is an inexhaustible positive principle—which is the first power in Nature. But an unseen power turns everything that appears in the world back into an endless circle. The cause of this is a negative principle that returns all things to their source—which is the second power in Nature. The idea of these two powers, in conflict but forming a unity, leads to the conception of an organising Principle which makes the world

into a system. It was perhaps this which the ancients meant when they spoke of the World-Soul.[1]

In his Preface to *The World-Soul*, Schelling gives this description of the ultimate Living Reality:

> The living Entity, therefore, continues its own self-circumscribed existence, engendering the unique, transforming so as to mirror the eternal in the temporal; while itself the strength, content and structure of all forms, makes Time into its own Eternity, and is *untouched by any change* (p. 373–4. italics mine).

The respect in which Schelling's conception is unrepresentative of the climate of opinion of his day, though his own ideas have obviously been affected by it, is that he makes a distinction between the world-process and its Cause; and maintains (not without laying himself open to very damaging objections) that, while somehow itself part of change, it is nevertheless 'untouched by any change—von keinem Wechsel berührt wird'.[2]

At the other end of the spectrum was the generally held view that 'Nature' was in fact everything; the universal cosmic Process, in itself both cause and effect. The best illustration of this is probably to be found in a famous article 'Nature: a Fragment', which appeared anonymously in 1783 in a magazine, the *Tierfurter Journal*. It was in fact written by a certain Georg Christoph Tobler; but it was at the time, and for long afterwards, attributed to Goethe. Forty-five years later, Goethe wrote a 'Comment', pointing out in what respects it fell short of his own conceptions, to which we must return. The 'Nature Fragment', which has been called a 'hymn', is certainly rather of the nature of poetry, not to say rhapsody, than philosophy. A few extracts will illustrate:

She (Nature) is forever creating new forms; that which now

---

[1] *Von der Weltseele*, 1798. Collected edn. of Schelling's works, Stuttgart and Augsburg, 1857, vol. 2, p. 381. The original of the vital sentence reads 'Diese beiden streitenden Kräfte zugleich in der Einheit und im Conflikt System bildenden Princips'.

[2] Schelling's application of idealistic philosophical analysis to what we regard as purely scientific matters makes curious reading today; e.g. the chapter on 'The Philosophy of Chemistry' in *Ideas for a Philosophy of Nature*, 1858 edn., (vol. 2, p. 257 *seq.*)

is has never been before, that which was does not come again—
everything is new, and yet always the old.

In her there is perpetual living, becoming and moving, and
yet she progresses no further. She is eternally transforming
herself, and there is not a moment of immobility in her. Of the
immutable she has no conception, and she has laid her curse on
immobility.

Her spectacle is forever new, because she is continually
creating new spectators. Life is her most beautiful invention;
and death is her artifice for having abundant life.

She is everything. She is her own reward and her own
punishment, her own joy and her own torment. She is harsh
and gentle, lovable and terrifying, powerless and immeasurably
powerful. Everything exists for ever in her. She knows
nothing of past and future. The present is her eternity.

As can be seen from the above sufficiently representative
examples, this famous 'Fragment' is neither a piece of reasoned
argument, nor a prose poem with any recognisable structure, but
rather a random collection of oracular utterances which sometimes transcend the limits of intelligibility (e.g. 'she is her own
reward and her own punishment'). Nevertheless, despite appear-
ances, it is something more significant than a stream of paradoxes;
it was very characteristic of its day and age; and two comments
must be made upon it.

The first is that here there is no question of anything other
than, or beyond or behind, 'Nature' herself. She is not, as is the
Spirit of Earth in *Faust*, something which weaves 'the garment of
God', the outward material manifestation of an inner spiritual
reality. Nor is she, as in Schelling's theory, the continually
becoming Effect of a Cause that is itself changeless. She herself
is all life, conceived as one universal, indivisible entity. 'Everything exists for ever in her'. There is no question of Deity,
whether immanent or transcendent. The second comment to be
made is that here there is no question of anything that could be
called Progress, only Process, eternally continuing but having no
direction. We are told, it is true, that Nature continually creates
what was not there before. But there is no trace of suggestion
that the new creation in any way represents any advance upon the
old. It was precisely this last point which Goethe made in his
'Comment', of which more anon. The author of the *Nature*

Fragment had nothing of the scientist in him; and had no conception of anything in Nature such as adaptation of means to ends; which, as we shall see, Goethe certainly did have. In view of the power and range of Goethe's mind, it seems strange to us that he should have been thought to be the author of something so intellectually flaccid as the *Nature Fragment*.

The great English author, whose name immediately comes to mind as our best-known representative of the Nature 'pantheists' of the later eighteenth century, has already several times been mentioned and quoted. It is, of course, Wordsworth. The number of books on Wordsworth continues to grow; and of those devoted to his 'philosophy', the latest is perhaps the best.[1] It certainly leaves nothing much more to be investigated; and proves pretty conclusively that the investigation can add little, if anything, to our knowledge and appreciation of the essential Wordsworth. As another recent writer on Wordsworth very pertinently reminds us:

> Matthew Arnold, in the introduction to his selection of Wordsworth's poetry, makes a point of warning readers against Wordsworthians who wish to find in Wordsworth a philosopher rather than a poet.
> 'Wordsworthians are apt to praise him for the wrong things, and to lay far too much stress upon what they call his philosophy. His poetry is the reality, his philosophy . . . the illusion.'[2]

Dr. Rader provides a most cogent illustration of this in his section devoted to Wordsworth and the conception of a World-Soul.[3] Such metaphysical speculations did, indeed, deeply interest Coleridge. But Wordsworth they left untouched. As E. de Selincourt, puts it:

> With Coleridge's attempt to fuse philosophy and religion he was wholly unconcerned. His philosophy, as far as he was a philosopher, *was* his religion; he never examined its logical implications, and any analysis that seemed to disturb its integrity he would have set down to 'that false secondary power by which we multiply distinctions', appealing against it to the

[1] Melvin Rader: *Wordsworth, a philosophical approach.* Oxford, 1967.
[2] Alec King: *Wordsworth and the Artist's Vision.* London, 1966.
[3] Op. cit., II, 8.

C

tribunal of his own deepest experience. His faith was a passionate intuition of God present in the Universe and in the mind of Man; his philosophy no more than the struggle of his reason to account for it.[1]

None of Wordsworth's greatest and most characteristic poetry would have been different in any essential had he never heard of Plato, the neo-Platonists or Spinoza. The fundamental truth about Wordsworth and Nature can be stated simply: his was not a philosophical approach, but an emotional involvement—in de Selincourt's less contemporary language, a religion. And the consequence was that he was concerned, not primarily with metaphysical but with moral questions; not so much with what Nature *is* as with what she *does*; with the influence she exerts upon the heart, mind and character of the individual; and, in the first place, upon Wordsworth himself. This is the subject of *The Prelude, or Growth of a Poet's Mind*, to give its full title. Of innumerable examples from that poem, the best is probably the marvellous passage near the end of Book II, beginning:

> I felt the sentiment of Being spread
> O'er all that moves and all that seemeth still. . . .

and ending some 30 lines later:

> If in this time
> Of dereliction and dismay, I yet
> Despair not of our nature; but retain
> A more than Roman confidence, a faith
> That fails not, in all sorrows my support,
> The blessing of my life, the gift is yours,
> Ye mountains! Thine, O Nature! Thou hast fed
> My lofty speculations; and in thee,
> For this uneasy heart of ours, I find
> A never-failing principle of joy,
> And purest passion.[2]

So great a master of the English language did not here use the words 'heart' and 'passion' without knowing what he was doing.
The question of what Nature *is* arises for Wordsworth, in so

[1] Introduction to his *shorter* edn. of the 1805 *Prelude* (first published 1933).
[2] *Prelude*, Bk. II, 457 *seq.*

far as it does arise, directly from this matter of her power and authority. Only as he conceived her could she have the power to do what she does. In face of the overwhelming evidence, it cannot really be seriously denied that during the years when his genius was at its height (i.e. roughly the ten years around the turn of the eighteenth–nineteenth centuries), he was what is generally called a Pantheist in the Spinozan sense. Put in philosophical terms (he himself neither employed, nor thought in such terms), he felt what he called Nature to be immanent Deity; an over-powering sense that there is one universal Life, which manifests Itself in all individual lives:

> Great God!
> Who send'st thyself into this breathing world
> Through Nature and through every kind of life,
> And mak'st man what he is, Creature divine.[1]

That for Wordsworth, and it is one of his most recurrent and profoundest themes, Man at his best shares this immanence of Deity, is clear from an earlier passage:

> . . . to my Soul I say
> I recognise thy glory; in such strength
> Of usurpation, in such visitings
> Of awful promise, when the light of sense
> Goes out in flashes that have shown to us
> The invisible world, doth Greatness make abode,
> There harbours whether we be young or old.
> Our destiny, our nature, and our home
> Is with infinitude, and only there;
> With hope it is, hope that can never die,
> Effort, and expectation, and desire,
> And something evermore about to be.[2]

As he grew older, Wordsworth not only lost his early vision, which he bitterly regretted ('The things that I have seen I now can see no more'); he also became progressively more orthodox. Having been accused of confusing Nature, God's creation, with God Himself, his revisions of *The Prelude* during forty-five years

[1] *Prelude* X, 386–9.
[2] *Prelude* VI, 531–42

were largely devoted to removing this cause of offence. Fortunately for posterity, and his own fame, what he first wrote when his genius was at its zenith has not been lost. The clearest evidence of all as to Wordsworth's belief ('feeling' might be a more accurate word) at that time is to be found in lines which he then wrote, but never published. They were first published by E. de Selincourt in 1928, in his monumental edition of the 1805 version of *The Prelude*,[1] and its variants. He dates the manuscript notebook containing them 'between the summer of 1798 and February 1800'.[2] The passage is a fragment; and in it Wordsworth writes (his use of capital and lower-case letters is here reproduced):

> the one interior life...
> That lives in all things
> In which all beings live with god, themselves
> Are god, Existing in the mighty whole,
> As indistinguishable as the cloudless East
> At noon is from the cloudless West, when all
> The hemisphere is one cerulean blue.

What is probably the most quoted passage in all his poetry, which dates from just before, puts it thus:

> And I have felt
> A presence that disturbs me with the joy
> Of elevated thoughts; a sense sublime
> Of something far more deeply interfused,
> Whose dwelling is the light of setting suns,
> And the round ocean, and the living air,
> And the blue sky, and in the mind of man,
> A motion and a spirit, that impels
> All thinking things, all objects of all thought,
> And rolls through all things.[3]

Commenting on this passage, Dr. Rader writes:

The proper way to interpret the lines, I believe, is to regard them as *no more than a partial expression of pantheism*; the presence is not God, but a part of God. Besides the 'motion and the

[1] de Selincourt examines the revisions in detail.
[2] The 1928 edn. of *The Prelude*, pp. 512–3.
[3] 'Tintern Abbey,' 94–103.

spirit' there is the outward form of the world, or matter; but both spirit and body are ultimately included in the all-embracing unity which is God.[1]

This is surely a distinction without a difference. If Dr. Rader can write the sentence here italicised, and apply it to the lines quoted, it is not worth arguing about what is 'not God, but a part of God'; or asking what possible meaning can be assigned to 'a part' of an 'all-embracing unity'. It was during these wonderful years that one of the greatest of English poets had the supreme vision, granted him through Nature, of the one Life that lives in all things. He himself, describing his descent from the Simplon Pass, rightly calls it an Apocalypse; the revelation of That which is, which was, and which shall be hereafter:

> The immeasurable height
> Of woods decaying, never to be decayed,
> The stationary blasts of water-falls,
> And every where along the hollow rent
> Winds thwarting winds, bewildered and forlorn,
> The torrents shooting from the clear blue sky,
> The rocks that muttered close upon our ears,
> Black drizzling crags that spake by the way-side
> As if a voice were in them, the sick sight
> And giddy prospect of the raving stream,
> The unfettered clouds, and region of the Heavens,
> Tumult and peace, the darkness and the light
> Were all like workings of one mind, the features
> Of the same face, blossoms upon one tree,
> Characters of the great Apocalypse,
> The types and symbols of Eternity,
> Of first and last, and midst, and without end.[2]

---

[1] Op. cit. p. 60. Miss E. C. Batho (*The Later Wordsworth*, 1936) after reading W. R. Inge on Plotinus (as she acknowledges), says that it is more accurate to call this Tintern Abbey passage 'panentheism' rather than 'pantheism'. The point seems a minor one of terminology.

[2] *Prelude*, VI, 556–72. The inexplicable exclusion by A. King (op. cit. p. 64) of this passage from the 'creative vision' of the Prelude is as absurd as it is indefensible. That it expresses Wordsworth's most profound feelings there can be no question. Prof. King admits it to be 'early' (it dates from 1799) but says that it is 'consciously in the style of the Sublime School'. None of the Sublime School ever distantly approached such sublimity. E. de Selincourt has conclusively shown that it is deliberately Shakespearian. No finer example exists of Wordsworth's deliberate choice of high eloquence for a theme to which no lower key is adequate.

To say that what Wordsworth totally lacked was 'natural philosophy', sounds today so violently paradoxical as to seem outrageous. Nevertheless, were we using the language of his day, it would be no more than the simple truth. For the eighteenth century called 'natural philosophy' what we today call science; the old name, much older than the eighteenth century (it was the 'philosophia naturae' of the mediaeval universities), survives in the official title of some of the Chairs in British Universities and in the Philosophical Transactions of the Royal Society. As an undergraduate at Trinity College, Cambridge, Wordsworth had, indeed, been impressed by the monument to Newton; probably the most notable addition to the final (1850) version of the Prelude is the couplet describing it:

> The marble index of a mind forever
> Voyaging through strange seas of Thought, alone—[1]

But of what science essentially is and does, and of the scientific attitude of mind, he had virtually no conception; much less even than of metaphysics. That his own lifetime overlapped those of both Kant (1724–1804) and Hegel (1770–1831) made no difference whatever to his own views of Nature and the Universe. But it also overlapped the lifetime of at least half a dozen men who were among the Founding Fathers of modern science.[2] What they discovered about Nature and the Universe was of no more concern to him than if they had lived in another planet. Nature's revelation of Reality to the individual soul of man was, as we have seen, of the utmost moral importance to Wordsworth. But that Nature is herself a physical Process, of unimaginable scale and complexity, and with stupendous implications, he had little notion and less interest.[3]

In this he differed profoundly from Goethe. The great 'Sage of Weimar' was, as we have seen, already convinced in his early manhood that Nature was a Process, and that this Process was at the heart of the Universe. But this conviction rested upon much

---

[1] *Prelude III*, 62–3.

[2] To mention no others: Linnaeus (1707–78); Lavoisier (1743–94); Laplace (1749–1829); Cuvier (1769–1832); Humphry Davy (1778–1829; he was a friend of Coleridge); Faraday (1791–1867).

[3] In so far as he adopted a conscious attitude towards enquiry into natural processes, it was an anti-scientific one:
Our meddling intellect
Misshapes the beauteous forms of things;
We murder to dissect ('The Tables Turned,' 1798).

more than imaginative intuition. Few men in human history have had a mind so Protean. It is not easy to name any major activity of the human intelligence in which he showed no interest; of an astonishing number he had at least some first-hand technical knowledge as it was in his day.[1] His interests ranged from Optics, Physics and Geology to Anatomy and Morphology. During the 1790s he wrote a whole series of scientific papers, notably two: on the Metamorphoses of Plants, and of Animals. He even wrote a poem on each of these subjects; which, while they do not provide striking evidence of Goethe's power as a poet—there is plenty of that elsewhere—do show something of his mental quality. Here are two passages from the poem on Animals:

> Wagt ihr, also bereitet, die letzte Stufe zu steigen
> Dieses Gipfels, so reicht mir die Hand und öffnet den freien
> Blick ins weite Feld der Natur. Sie spendet die reichen
> Lebensgaben umher, die Göttin, aber empfindet
> Keine Sorge, wie sterbliche Fraun, um ihrer Gebornen
> Sichere Nahrung. . . .

> Zweck sein selbst ist jegliches Thier, vollkommen entspringt es
> Aus dem Schosz der Natur und zeugt vollkommene Kinder.
> Alle Glieder bilden sich aus nach ew'gen Gesetzen,
> Und die seltenste Form bewahrt im Geheimen das Urbild.
> So ist jeglicher Mund geschickt, die Speise zu fassen
> Welche dem Körper gebührt.[2]

Suffice it here to comment upon this, that, whatever scientific errors or omissions it may today seem to contain (it was written in or about 1806), it enunciates two principles of natural process which are among the cardinal principles of modern science:

[1] His day was the last in which this was even possible. The only notable exceptions were probably mathematics and music; and he would be a bold man who affirmed without fear of contradiction that Goethe knew nothing of either. Of the value of philosophy as a formal discipline he was sceptical. In his poem 'Die Weisen und die Leute', the people ask the fundamental questions, the philosophers giving them frivolous and superficial answers. It is the first of the subjects Faust laments having wasted his time on.

[2] If, thus prepared, you dare to climb the final step of this summit, give me your hand and gaze freely into the wide field of Nature. She is prodigal with her rich gifts of life, the Goddess; but she experiences no anxiety, as do mortal women, for the nurture of her children. . . . Each animal is designed to be an end in itself; it springs, perfect, from Nature's lap and begets perfect offspring. All limbs develop according to eternal laws, and the strangest shape secretly preserves the original design. Thus every mouth is fitted to take hold of the food which suits the body.

(i) Operation according to immutable and universal laws;
(ii) In a biological context, the adaptation of means to ends.

It was a mind of this quality which said:
'Nature is for ever at work, living, overflowing, prodigal;
so that the Unending may perpetually become the Present; for
nothing can linger unchanged.'[1]

Such a conception, upon the grandest possible scale, of the
Universe as Process, is the subject of one of his late, most characteristic, poems, 'Eins und Alles'. The first stanza describes the
delight of the individual at being able to lose himself, and all his
passions and desires, in the consciousness of being part of the
limitless Universe. The poem continues:

> Weltseele, komm uns zu durchdringen!
> Denn mit dem Weltgeist selbst zu ringen,
> Wird unserer Kräfte Hochberuf.
> Theilnehmend führen gute Geister,
> Gelinde leitend, höchste Meister,
> Zu dem, der alles schafft und schuf.
>
> Und umzuschaffen das Geschaffne,
> Damit sich's nicht zum Starren waffne,
> Wirkt ewiges, lebendiges Thun.
> Und was nicht war, nun will es werden,
> Zu reinen Sonnen, farbigen Erden,
> In keinem Falle darf es ruhn.
>
> Es soll sich regen, schaffend handeln,
> Erst sich gestalten, dann verwandeln;
> Nur scheinbar steh'ts Momente still.
> Das Ewige regt sich fort in allen;
> Denn alles muss in Nichts zerfallen,
> Wenn es im Seyn beharren will.[2]

---

[1] An observation quoted by Edward von der Hellen (Jubilee edition, Stuttgart
and Augsburg, 1902 *seq.*, vol. 2, p. 352).

[2] Written in 1821. The title, like that of the poem 'Weltseele', as also some of the
ideas, was almost certainly suggested by his reading of Schelling.
The One and the All.
Come, World-Soul, and penetrate us wholly. Then it will become the exalted
mission of our powers to strive with the World-Spirit. Benevolent spirits, supreme
masters, co-operating with us, gently lead us to him who created, and creates,
everything.

It cannot be too strongly emphasised that Goethe's conception of the Process in the Universe was *not* one of continued activity, going round in a circle—the puppy chasing its own tail. It was one of creative emergence, of that which never was coming into existence ('Und was nicht war, nun will es werden'), of Becoming; 'Das Werdende', to use the word which he puts into the mouth of God in the 'Prolog im Himmel'. This magnificent piece of poetry was neither in the *Ur-Faust*, nor in the Fragment of 1790; it first appeared in the First Edition of 1808. It was, of course, a deliberate imitation of the Book of Job; and the appearance of the Almighty as one of the *dramatis personae* is of no philosophical or religious significance, but simply a literary convention. One of the purposes of this Prolog is to contrast the positive principle behind all creation with the negative principle incarnate in Mephisto, the representative of 'the spirits that deny' ('von allen Geistern, die verneinen . . .'). Having given Mephisto permission to do what he asks with Faust, the Lord says to the Archangels:

> Doch ihr, die echten Göttersöhne,
> Erfreut euch der lebendig reichen Schöne!
> Das Werdende, das ewig wirkt und lebt,
> Umfass' euch mit der Liebe holden Schranken,
> Und was in schwankender Erscheinung schwebt,
> Befestiget mit dauernden Gedanken.[1]

It was during Goethe's lifetime, and particularly during his maturity and old age, that the nature and origin of the physical environment in which Man lives his terrestrial life, and also of Man himself, were increasingly coming under investigation of a sort which was new in human history. What made it new was its

---

Everlasting, living action is directed to transforming all created things so that they do not obtain the power to remain unchanged. That which was not now desires to become—pure suns, many-coloured worlds; under no circumstances can it remain at rest.

It must bestir itself, act creatively, first assuming form, and then changing; only in appearance does it momentarily remain still. The Eternal continually embodies Itself in everything; for everything must pass by the way of annihilation if there is to be continuing existence.

The essential difference from Schelling is that, for Goethe, everything that exists, not merely the Effects, excluding the Cause, is involved in Change and Process.

[1] 344–9: But ye, the true sons of God, rejoice in the living, rich Beauty! May That-which-becomes, which eternally works and lives, embrace you in the fair bonds of love. That which hovers in swaying appearance make ye fast with enduring thoughts.

increasingly scientific character as the evidence on which it was built accumulated. The results tended to be formulated in general theories, impressive in their comprehensiveness even though they have since proved to be either false, or at best much too sweeping. The two great examples are the 'Nebular Hypothesis' of Laplace, the great mathematician and astronomer; and the theory of organic evolution famous during the nineteenth century under the name 'Lamarckism'. More must be said of them in the next chapter; and the full developments of both were published somewhat later. But the essential, fundamental conceptions of each of them appeared before the first edition of *Faust*.[1] As far as it can be stated in one sentence, the common conclusion to be drawn from both is this: all organic life on this planet, and the planet itself and the whole solar and stellar system to which it belongs, are the result of development, of Process.

By 1805 Goethe had written a poem which is perhaps the most illuminating commentary that will ever be made upon God's use, in the Prolog im Himmel, of the expression 'Das Werdende'. Its subject is the Cosmic Process, which is the inner life of the Universe. Here are the third and fourth stanzas of 'Weltseele':

> Dann treibt ihr euch, gewaltige Kometen,
> Ins Weit' und Weitr' hinan.
> Das Labyrinth der Sonnen und Planeten
> Durchschneidet eure Bahn.

> Ihr greifet rasch nach ungeformten Erden
> Und wirket schöpfrisch jung,
> Dass sie belebt und stets belebter werden
> Im abgemessnen Schwung.[2]

The word 'Evolution' goes back at least to the early seventeenth century and even in several technical senses as well as the general basic one of: 'The process of evolving, unrolling, opening

---

[1] Laplace: A note in *Exposition du système du monde*, 1796. Lamarck: *Système des animaux sans vertèbres*—a foretaste of the great work of 1815.

[2] Then you, ye mighty comets, drive further and further into space. Your orbit cuts across the labyrinth of suns and planets. You reach out rapidly towards worlds as yet unformed, and exert your young creative action so that they may become inhabited and increasingly filled with life according to the preordained rhythm. The poem as a whole is untranslatable; the most careful paraphrase could give but a very imperfect idea of it. The reference to comets may make worth mentioning Schelling's discussion of whether their nuclei are solid or gaseous.

out or disengaging from an envelope'.[1] The one further sense, which arose in the nineteenth century, is thus defined: 'The origination of species conceived as a process of development from earlier forms, and not as due to "special creation".' Into this we must enquire in the next chapter. Questions concerning the origin of species and the ancestry of Man were hardly beginning to be asked by the end of Goethe's lifetime. The tremendous controversies which they were to produce still lay a quarter of a century in the future when he died. Bearing in mind the important exception just mentioned, it can, however, confidently be claimed that Goethe was one of the earliest, as he certainly was one of the greatest apostles of what, when used of him, can fairly be called the Gospel of Evolution; and it can justly be so called, because to him the Cosmic Process implied Advance; not only from the simple to the complex, but also from the lower to the higher. His own favourite and characteristic word for it, 'Steigerung', contains this spatial metaphor; for it derives from the verb 'steigen', to rise or climb.[2]

Earlier in this chapter, some quotations were given from the famous *Nature Fragment* of 1783, which many at the time attributed to Goethe. In May 1828, less than four years before he died, Goethe made the following 'Comment' upon it (as can be seen by reference to the German, the word 'Steigerung' is here rendered 'Ascent'):

> I can no longer in fact remember having written these meditations, only they agree well with conceptions to which my mind had at that time attained.
>
> The completion, however, which is lacking is the conception of two great driving forces in all Nature: the idea of polarity, and of ascent; the former being characteristic of Matter, in so far as we conceive it to be physical, the latter in so far as we conceive it to be spiritual; the former manifested in perpetual attraction and repulsion, the latter in a perpetual urge upwards. Since, however, Matter has no effective existence without Spirit, nor Spirit without Matter, the material world is capable of an upward urge just as the spiritual cannot be denied the capacity of attraction and repulsion. Only he who has sufficiently analysed to be able to effect a synthesis, and sufficiently

[margin note: Polarity and ascent]

---

[1] New English Dictionary.

[2] A complete Goethe dictionary is in process of publication. A recent reviewer in the Times Literary Supplement lamented that he would not live to see the entry for 'Steigerung'.

synthesised to be capable of analysis, is capable of conceiving this.[1]

The conception that the material and the spiritual are inextricably bound up with each other, and are, indeed, different aspects of the one underlying Reality, is one that grew upon Goethe with advancing years. It finds its ultimate expression at the end of the Second Part of *Faust*, in the words of the Chorus mysticus:

> Alles Vergängliche
> Ist nur ein Gleichniss;
> Das Unzulängliche,
> Hier wird's Ereigniss.[2]

How he conceived the relationship between Deity, and the Universe in which It is immanent, is perhaps best expressed in the poem 'Proaemion', which Goethe prefixed to the section of his collected poems which he entitled 'Gott und Welt':

> Was wär' ein Gott, der nur von aussen stiesse,
> Im Kreis das All am Finger laufen liesse,
> Ihm ziemt's, die Welt im Innern zu bewegen,
> Natur in Sich, Sich in Natur zu hegen,
> So dass, was in Ihm lebt und webt und ist,
> Nie seine Kraft, nie Seinen Geist vermisst.[3]

---

[1] The text of this Fragment is to be found in the two modern editions of Goethe: Hamburgerausgabe (1955), vol. 13, pp. 45–7, with Goethe's 'Erläuterung', pp. 48–9; cf notes on pp. 571–2; Insel Ausgabe 1965, vol. 16, pp. 921–4, with the 'Erläuterung' on pp. 925–6; cf also p. 978. There is, in the former edition, a short bibliography of the Fragment. The following is the text of Goethe's Comment (dated Weimar, 24th May 1828).

Dass ich diese Betrachtungen verfasst, kann ich mich faktisch zwar nicht erinnern, allein sie stimmen mit den Vorstellungen wohl überein, zu denen sich mein Geist damals ausgebildet hatte.

Die Erfüllung aber, die (ihm) fehlt, ist die Anschauung der zwei grossen Triebräder aller Natur: der Begriff von Polarität und von Steigerung, jene der Materie, insofern wir sie materiell, diese ihr dagegen, insofern wir sie geistig denken, angehörig; jene ist im immerwährenden Anziehen und Abstossen, diese im immerstrebenden Aufsteigen. Weil aber die Materie nie ohne Geist, der Geist nie ohne Materie, existiert und wirksam sein kann, so vermag auch die Materie sich zu steigern, so wie's sich der Geist nicht nehmen lässt, anzuziehen und abzustossen; wie derjenige nur allein zu denken vermag, der genugsam getrennt hat, um zu verbinden, genugsam verbunden hat, um wieder trennen zu mögen.

[2] Everything transitory is but an image. The unattainable here becomes achievement.

[3] What would a God be Who only intervened from without, Who left the Universe to revolve in a circle about His finger? It becomes Him to move the world from within; to foster Nature within Himself and Himself within Nature; so that what lives and moves and exists in Him never lacks His power and His spirit.

CHAPTER TWO

THE THEORY OF EVOLUTION IN ENGLISH POETRY

We have seen how, by the time of Goethe's death in 1832, one of the foremost minds of the modern world had become firmly convinced that the entire Universe was the result of the operation of a continuing evolutionary Process. A few words must now be said about something which was fundamental to such a conception, viz., the idea of Universal Law. It must at once be added that the reference is not to moral law, but to what had by the seventeenth century come to be known as 'Natural Law', to which all the physical phenomena of the Universe are subject. Essentially a product of the Renaissance (which owed the germ of it to the Greeks, who were the founders of Western civilization), this was strengthened and deepened by all the great scientists from at least Copernicus onwards; and perhaps most of all by Sir Isaac Newton, with his demonstration of the universal operation of the force of gravity according to the laws of mathematics.[1] The universal operation of Natural Law was also an essential and integral part of Spinoza's conception of one Cosmic Reality. As the quotation already given from the poem on the Metamorphoses of Animals shows, Goethe shared this conception. One of his most famous poems applies the same idea to human life:

> Nach ewigen, ehrnen,
> Grossen Gesetzen
> Müssen wir alle
> Unseres Daseyns
> Kreise vollenden.[2]

As the nineteenth century advanced, belief in the immediate operation and special intervention of an Almighty Power transcendent to the Universe ('ein Gott, der nur von aussen stiesse'),

---

[1] Newton's magnum opus, *Philosophiae Naturalis Principia Mathematica* was published in 1687. It was, of course, from mathematics that there first arose the conception of the universal operation of natural law.

[2] In accordance with eternal, venerable, mighty laws we must all complete the circle of our existence ('Das Göttliche'). As the context shows, Goethe was here thinking of moral as well as natural law; he made no dichotomy between them.

became more and more difficult to hold; and this conception of operation through universal law began to replace such belief. The point may be illustrated by two quotations from the third Bridgwater Treatise,[1] published in 1833, by William Whewell, Professor of Mineralogy at Cambridge 1828–1832. He was Tennyson's tutor, and became Master of Trinity in 1841. In this treatise Whewell wrote:

> God is the author and governor of the Universe through the laws which He has given to its parts, the properties which He has impressed upon its constituent elements.

And again:

> The laws of material Nature, such as we have described them, operate at all times and in all places; affect every province of the Universe and involve every relation of its parts.[2]

It would not be difficult to add further quotations to the same effect from the writings of other scientists and philosophers of the period, e.g. from Herschel's *On the Study of Natural Philosophy* (1830).[3]

In the previous chapter, the words of three great creative writers were used to illustrate the emergence of a new conception of the Universe. In the nineteenth century, this conception, reinforced by an ever-increasing flood of scientific discovery, became overwhelming; until, just after the middle of the century, it came to a head-on collision with the teaching, as then interpreted, of orthodox religion. There is one English poet who probably illustrates this better than any other European author. That poet is Alfred Tennyson (1809–92). While not of the stature of Goethe, it can hardly be denied that no poet is more certain of a secure place in the history of English literature. Apart altogether from questions of taste and fashion in poetry, historical reasons

[1] These Treatises, of which eight in all appeared between 1833 and 1836, were the result of a legacy given to the British Museum by the eighth Earl of Bridgwater for the best work 'On the Power, Wisdom and Goodness of God, as manifested in the Creation'. Belonging essentially to the literature of apologetics, they vary in quality; but some knowledge of them is indispensable to any student of the period.
[2] P. 361.
[3] The article on Herschel in the *Encyclopedia Britannica* says of this work that it 'possesses an interest which no future advances of the subjects on which he wrote can obliterate'.

alone would seem to assure him of such a place. He belonged to one of the crucial ages of modern civilisation; and, among all the English writers of that age, he was perhaps the most representative. No poet of equal rank has ever been more dominated by an idea than was Tennyson by the idea of Evolution, taking the word in its wider philosophical, and not merely its biological sense. The certainty of 'la somma sapienza e'l primo amore' was not more essential to Dante's vision of Hell and Heaven, the conviction of human freewill was not more fundamental to Milton's justification of the ways of God, than was the belief in an evolutionary Process necessary to Tennyson's whole conception of the nature and meaning of the Universe.

None of the other Victorian poets bears any comparison with him in this respect. Their interests all lay elsewhere. Browning was above all interested in Personality, human and divine; of science he took but scant notice. There are a few passages, notably at the end of 'Paracelsus', and in 'Cleon', which, it has been claimed, owe something to the 'evolutionary' atmosphere of the age. But the only passage in all Browning's poetry of which this can be said with any confidence is one in the late, and rather disappointing 'Prince Hohenstiel-Schwangau'. This dates from the same year as Darwin's *Descent of Man* (1871); and in it, the Prince, who is intended to be the deposed and exiled Napoleon III, as well as referring to the Ice Age and to the Earth's volcanic past, makes a deliberate allusion to Darwin:

> 'Will you have why and wherefore, and the fact
> Made plain as pikestaff?' modern Science asks.
> 'That mass man sprung from was a jelly-lump
> Once on a time; he kept an after course
> Through fish and insect, reptile, bird and beast,
> Till he attained to be an ape at last,
> Or last but one. And if this doctrine shock
> In aught the natural pride. . . .'

It is no more than a passing, and isolated, allusion to something which was at the time the subject of violent public controversy.[1] For any fundamental effect that the evolutionary science of his

[1] In *Dramatis Personae* in 1864, he had made just such a contemporary allusion to the controversy over *Essays and Reviews* (in the poem 'Gold Hair').

century had upon Browning, he might have been living in another. Matthew Arnold was antipathetic to science, and disillusioned with religion. Admirer of Wordsworth and Goethe though he was, his pessimistic, stoic humanism had as little of the 'Roman confidence' of the one as it had of the Promethean versatility of the other. And such knowledge of the Universe as his generation discovered only filled him with sadness. For him, as he said of his contemporaries, the sea of Faith had ebbed, and left only

> Its melancholy, long withdrawing roar.[1]

Swinburne, indeed, underwent the influence of his age, though of science and all its works he knew nothing whatever and cared less. In his case, the strange and quite unexpected result was a passionate discipleship, at least for a time, to the 'Religion of Humanity'; which must form the subject of another chapter.

For being 'the poet of Science' Tennyson has been both praised and blamed; but only A. C. Bradley seems to have expressed the simple truth:

> With the partial exception of Shelley, Tennyson is the only one of our great poets whose attitude towards the sciences of Nature was what a modern poet's attitude ought to be. . . . the only one to whose habitual way of seeing, imagining and thinking it makes any real difference that Laplace, or for that matter Copernicus, ever lived.[2]

A scientist, who himself played a part in the turmoils of the later nineteenth century, best described what Tennyson meant to his contemporaries, at a time when the fierce dispute between the scientist and the theologian shook intellectual Europe:

> In the conflict between Science and Faith our business was to accept the one without rejecting the other; and that he achieved. Never did his acceptance of the animal ancestry of man, for instance, upset his belief in the essential divinity of the human soul, its immortality, its supremacy, its eternal destiny.[3]

[1] 'Dover Beach.'
[2] 'The reaction against Tennyson' (in *A Miscellany*).
[3] 'The attitude of Tennyson towards Science', by Sir Oliver Lodge, in *Tennyson and his Friends*, ed. H. Tennyson (1911).

And even that is only half the truth. For the real interest and significance of Tennyson's position is this: not only did he accept scientific truth without losing religious faith; the truths of science became to him an essential part of the truth of faith. This ought not to be without interest to the twentieth century, which has reaped the harvest that the nineteenth sowed.

The fundamental link between the thought of Tennyson and the science of the nineteenth century is to be found in the idea of Process, whose earlier stages in the eighteenth century we have been considering. The prodigious development and ever-increasing application of the conception of Process was surely one of the most remarkable achievements in the whole history of human thought. If we substitute the word 'Evolution' for the word 'Process', this will be at once conceded. But, as has already been pointed out, the word 'Evolution' acquired during the nineteenth century a new specialised, and therefore more limited, meaning; and this latter has associations which obscure the argument. In particular, it has become equated with the name of Charles Darwin. The name of Darwin, however, is only a source of error and confusion to the student of Tennyson. For Tennyson was Darwin's exact contemporary; and when *The Origin of Species* appeared at the end of 1859, the poet had been pondering the subject of Evolution as deeply and as long as the biologist himself, if not exactly from the same angle. It is possible that the word 'Evolution' came into Tennyson's poetry as a result of Darwin's book, though not necessarily, since it had been current, if not common, since the seventeenth century.[1] The conception of an evolutionary Process, however, had long occupied the foremost place there. Moreover, the evidence suggests that Tennyson's first acquaintance with this conception came, not from biology, but from astronomy. We have seen how Goethe could express it in an astronomical context.

On the subject of Tennyson's intimate knowledge of astronomy a bulky pamphlet could be written.[2] It is even possible exactly to date some of his poems by their astronomical references. Astronomy was the first science to interest Tennyson. To

---

[1] I know of no Tennyson dictionary which would enable this point to be determined.

[2] Much evidence is given in two papers entitled 'Astronomy in Tennyson', by C. T. Whitmell, in the *Journal* and *Transactions of the Leeds Astronomical Society* for 1906.

take only two examples from his early verse: 'The Devil and the Lady', written when he was fourteen,[1] contains a truly astonishing passage, the long speech in the second act, in which the Devil apostrophises the starry heavens. And in 'Timbuctoo', with which he gained the Chancellor's Medal for an English poem at Cambridge in 1829, there is a significant anticipation of his later scientific imagery:

> The clear galaxy,
> Shorn of its hoary lustre, wonderful,
> Distinct and vivid with sharp points of light,
> Blaze within blaze, an unimagined depth
> And harmony of planet-girdled suns
> And moon-encircled planets, wheel in wheel,
> Arch'd the wan sapphire.

For our present purpose, the most significant of the astronomical references in Tennyson's early poetry is to be found in 'The Palace of Art', written in or just before 1832. Some of the original stanzas were omitted from the volume published in that year, but were printed in the *Memoir*. Here are two of them:

> Hither, where all the deep unsounded skies
>   Shuddered with silent stars, she clomb,
> And as with optic glasses her keen eyes
>   Pierced through the mystic dome.

> *Regions of lucid matter taking forms,*
>   Brushes of fire, hazy gleams,
> Clusters and beds of worlds, and bee-like swarms
>   Of suns, and starry streams.

The line here italicised clearly contains the conception of Cosmic Process: the whole stanza can only refer to the Nebular hypothesis, which was first propounded by Laplace in 1796. The *locus classicus* in Tennyson for the Nebular hypothesis is, of course, in *The Princess*:

> This world was once a fluid haze of light,
> Till toward the centre set the starry tides,

[1] First published in 1930, edited by the poet's grandson.

> And eddied into suns, that wheeling cast
> The planets; then the monster, then the man.

It is particularly to be noted that here the Nebular hypothesis leads directly to that of biological evolution. Yet at least fifteen years before he wrote *The Princess*, and while still in his early twenties, Tennyson made the same connection in *The Palace of Art*. That poem would be notable enough if the only reference in it to the Cosmic Process were an astronomical one. But two more of the cancelled stanzas contain a biological conception of Cosmic Process which, considering the date and the age of the author, is remarkable:

> 'From shape to shape at first within the womb
>   'The brain is moulded', she began,
> And through all phases of all thought I come
>   Unto the perfect man.

> 'All nature widens upward. Evermore
>   The simpler essence lower lies,
> More complex is more perfect, owning more
>   Discourse, more widely wise.'

There we have the conception of biological evolution in connection with the human race, and with the individual man, expressed in terms of a science in which we should least expect a young poet to be interested, the science of Embryology. To the subject of foetal development here raised we will shortly return. Suffice it to remark in passing that the subject here introduced by Tennyson into the poem did not receive its accepted scientific formulation till more than thirty years after the poem was written.

The increase of knowledge has removed us so far from the Renaissance ideal of Humanism, that no student of literature can now be expected to be familiar with the history of science. This is very clear from the vague references made to Tennyson's connection with the theory of Evolution, not, indeed, by those so ignorant as to think him the follower of Darwin, but even by trained scholars, who knew that he anticipated Darwin, but knew nothing more. In view of this general vagueness, some brief explanation of the condition of scientific thought in Tennyson's

First the attack upon geocentrism, (17th Cent.) then upon anthropocentrism (18th cent.)

34   THE BECOMING OF GOD

youth seems necessary. In the light of that knowledge, it is possible to understand how, and why, Tennyson was deeply influenced by it; and what he meant when he wrote of himself, in the first 'Locksley Hall':

> Here about the beach I wandered, nourishing a youth sublime
> With the fairy tales of science, and the long result of time.

anthropocentric attack:

At the beginning of our first chapter, we saw how, by the middle of the seventeenth century, scientific discovery had made untenable the geocentric hypothesis of the Earth as the middle of the solar and stellar systems. Upon the anthropocentric hypothesis of the place occupied by Man in terrestrial life, no serious assault was made until the latter half of the eighteenth century. It arose in the first place from human curiosity as to Man's fellow denizens of our planet. Natural philosophers asked the momentous question: What are species? The first step towards answering it was to reduce the innumerable and bewildering abundance of living organisms to some system of scientific classification. This was chiefly done by the great Swedish naturalist Linnaeus (1707–78), who invented binary nomenclature.

(1) Classification of species.

Linnaeus himself went no further towards answering the question: What are species? He believed, as men had always done, that there are as many different species as there were different forms of life created at the beginning by the Almighty ('Species tot sunt diversae quot diversas formas ab initio creavit infinitum Ens'). But even Linnaeus himself recognised that additional new species may since have arisen, and may indeed still arise, by hybridism. A very great step further was taken by Georges Cuvier (1769–1832), the founder of Comparative Anatomy. It was Cuvier who discovered the division of animals into natural families. Conclusions similar to those of Cuvier were reached from independent investigations in Embryology carried out by Karl Ernst von Baer.[1] Von Baer's investigations had also another interest, of which more hereafter.

(2)

Cuvier, however, was not only interested in the present forms of life on Earth. He was also a great palaeontologist. With the evidence supplied by geology, he investigated the forms of life

[1] Von Baer's *Entwicklungsgeschichte der Thiere* (1828) contains the formulation of conclusions reached and stated in 1824.

which had formerly existed on the planet; and this led him to the assertion that the difference between living and extinct species increases, in proportion to the depth at which the remains of the latter are found, i.e. to their age in geological time. Hence he believed that one and the same species were never found in two succeeding strata; and from this he deduced that each geological epoch had possessed its own flora and fauna, divided, like the present, into many species (which he did not suspect of being anything but immutable). His final deduction was that each geological epoch had been destroyed by a cataclysm, and a new one created. He also pointed out that the active forces of nature as we now know them are not sufficient to account for the cataclysms demanded by his hypothesis, and that therefore the past history of the Earth had witnessed the operation of forces of which we can have but a faint conception.

The last Act of Shelley's *Prometheus Unbound* (1819) contains a remarkable passage; which is, however, much less extraordinary as evidence of Shelley's acquaintance with the 'cataclysmic' theory than it would be as the pure product of his own imagination, powerful though that was. Ione and Panthea are describing to each other the physical transformation of the Earth, resulting from the overthrow of Jupiter and the liberation of Prometheus by Demogorgon. Near the end of Panthea's last speech she says this:

                    The beams flash on
And make appear the melancholy ruins
Of cancelled cycles; anchors, beaks of ships;
Planks turned to marble; quivers, helms and spears,
And gorgon-headed targes, and the wheels
Of scythèd chariots, and the emblazonry
Of trophies, standards and armorial beasts
Round which death laughed, sepulchrèd emblems
Of dead destruction, ruin within ruin!
The wrecks beside of many a city vast,
Whose population which the earth grew over
Was mortal, but not human; see, they lie,
Their monstrous works, and uncouth skeletons,
Their statues, homes and fanes; prodigious shapes
Huddled in grey annihilation, split

Jammed in the hard, black deep; and over these,
The anatomies of unknown winged things,
And fishes which were isles of living scale,
And serpents, bony chains, twisted around
The iron crags; and over these
The jagged alligator, and the might
Of earth-convulsing behemoth, which once
Were monarch beasts, and on the slimy shores
And weed-overgrown continents of earth,
Increased and multiplied like summer worms
On an abandoned corpse, till the blue globe
Wrapt deluge round it like a cloak, and they
Yelled, gasped, and were abolished. . . .

Of that it need only be said that it could not have been written without some acquaintance with the geological and palaeonto-logical literature of the half century preceding the publication of *Prometheus Unbound*. It must, however, be added that neither this passage, nor any other in Shelley's poetry, provides evidence that he had any belief in Cosmic Process as the inner Reality of the Universe. Had he lived beyond his thirty-first year, and into the period when science was advancing from the views of Erasmus Darwin (whom Shelley certainly read) to those of his grandson Charles, he might possibly have come to it. But it is doubtful. Despite his undoubted knowledge of much of the science of his day, Shelley's whole cast of mind was not that of the scientist, but that of the idealist. The physical transformations of the material world were to him, during his short life-time, and would probably always have remained, of infinitely smaller significance than the eternal world of Ideas; which, for the Platonist, are the only lasting Reality. In the words of his incomparable elegy on Keats:

The one remains, the many change and pass;
Heaven's light for ever shines, Earth's shadows fly;
Life, like a dome of many-coloured glass,
Stains the white radiance of eternity. . . .

To return to more mundane matters: Cuvier's hypothesis as to the past history of terrestrial life held within it the germ of a momentous controversy. There is a striking reference to Cuvier's theory in *In Memoriam*, cxviii:

> They say
> The solid earth whereon we tread
> In tracts of fluent heat began,
> And grew to seeming-random forms,
> The seeming prey of cyclic storms.

In the first half of the nineteenth century this theory was widely held. It was believed that the past history of the Earth had consisted of a series of distinct phases; which necessarily involved the corollary of a belief in 'special creation' to account for them.

The theory of 'special creation', however, involved many great difficulties. It began to appear that some species which had existed in earlier epochs had vanished, only to be replaced by others, distinct indeed, but very similar; while some had not vanished, but continued to the present day. By the second quarter of the century, these facts had so shaken the 'special creation' theory that, as one writer put it:

> The inference from the facts and doctrines of this school (of 'special creation') is, that Divine Power has seen fit to change the species of elephants, rhinoceroses, tigers and bears, using special miracles to introduce new ones, with perhaps an additional tooth, another with a new tubercle or cusp on the third molar, while It has seen no occasion for a similar interference with the otter, wild cat and badger.[1]

An even greater difficulty was presented by the minor variations in species in isolated parts of the globe. Of these, the writer just quoted said:

> In the single fact that it necessitates a special fiat of the inconceivable Author of this sand cloud of worlds *to produce the flora of St. Helena*, we read the more than sufficient condemnation of the theory of special creation.

Already towards the end of the eighteenth century an altogether different hypothesis had begun to be put forward to

---

[1] *Explanations: a Sequel to Vestiges of the Natural History of Creation*, 1845, p. 155. The author of both books, Robert Chambers, was not identified till long afterwards.

account for the known variation of past and present forms of life. According to this, the diverse forms of terrestrial life were not distinctly and specially created, but were connected with one another by a process of development. As is the case with most of the greatest discoveries of the human mind, it seems impossible to isolate the first beginning of the theory of development. Like most ideas, it seems to have been in the air at a certain period; and it appears in many minds almost simultaneously.

The great scientist who has established the foremost claim to be for ever remembered, in connection with the theory of development, is Lamarck (1744–1829). It is perhaps not meticulously accurate to say that he was the founder of the Theory of Evolution; but no one can prove the title of any earlier claimant. Anyone at all familiar with the philosophical or theological discussions of the science of the early nineteenth century will know how frequently the term 'Lamarckism' appears in them. Lamarck's life-work was the investigation of the Invertebrata (it was he who introduced the term, applying it to what Linnaeus had called 'vermes'). His views on evolution appeared in a series of publications beginning in 1801 with *Système des animaux sans vertèbres*, and culminating in his magnum opus *Histoire naturelle des animaux sans vertèbres* (1815). Lamarck laid down four general laws governing the whole organisation of animals; which amount to the Theory of Evolution. The fourth of them postulates the inheritance of acquired characteristics; which has been the subject of controversy until the twentieth century. It is now generally abandoned. But the essence of the Theory of Evolution remains. The great contribution which Charles Darwin made to it, besides his lucid and cogent formulation, was his own theory of Natural Selection, and the vast mass of evidence upon which it was based. Darwin had arrived at his theory as early as 1844; but he continued to amass evidence until the independent discoveries of Alfred Wallace forced him to publish *The Origin of Species* in 1859.[1]

In the first quarter of the nineteenth century, while Lamarck was drawing such epoch-making conclusions from the study of invertebrate creatures, a systematic and little less epoch-making investigation was being made into the embryonic forms of life in animals and

[1] The book's subtitle was *The Preservation of Favoured Races in the Struggle for Life.* In ch. 3 Darwin quotes the famous phrase, originally coined by Herbert Spencer, 'the survival of the fittest'.

in Man. Ever since John Hunter (1728–93) had formed the great
collection of specimens which found its final home in the Royal
College of Surgeons, the embryo had been a subject of increasing
interest to physiologists. The systematic investigation carried out
at the beginning of the nineteenth century is chiefly associated
with the names of three embryologists: Friedrich Tiedemann,
E. A. R. Serres, and K. E. von Baer. It seems to have been
Tiedemann who first stated the most significant fact. He found
that the brain of the foetus, in the highest class of vertebrates,
assumes in succession a remarkable resemblance to the forms
which belong to fishes, reptiles and birds; so that in the passage
from the embryo to the perfect mammal there is a kind of typical
representation of all the transformations which more primitive
species underwent. Tiedemann and the early embryologists were,
indeed, under the impression that the resemblance was actual
identity. The work in which these conclusions were stated was
published at Nüremberg in 1816; and translated into English in
1826.[1]

It was in a translation of a German treatise on a highly
specialised branch of medical science that these conclusions
became available in English when Tennyson was fifteen. We are
told in the *Memoir* that he and his friends at Cambridge took
interest in the subject of the development of the human brain.[2] It
was before 1832 that Tennyson wrote:

> 'From shape to shape at first within the womb
>   "The brain is moulded," she began,
> And through all phases of all thought I come
>   Unto the perfect man.'

Meanwhile the investigation of the Cosmic Process was
proceeding in the other sciences, especially in geology. Cuvier's
hypothesis of cataclysms was destroyed by Sir Charles Lyell, who,
in his *Principles of Geology* (1830–3), showed that no cataclysms
were necessary to account for the terrestrial conditions of the
past revealed by geological evidence. The book was described by

---

[1] *Anatomie und Bildungsgeschichte des Gehirns im Foetus des Menschen nebst einer ver-
gleichenden Darstellung des Hirnbaues in den Thieren; Anatomy of the Foetal Brain with a
Comparative Exposition of its Structure in Animals* (Edinburgh, 1826). Serre's work was
entitled *Anatomie comparative du cerveau* (1824).

[2] Vol. I, p. 44.

its author as 'An Attempt to explain the former changes of the Earth's surface by references to causes now in operation'. It is an impressive account of that ceaseless process which has made the surface of our Earth what it now is. Of particular interest are the tenth and eleventh chapters of the first volume, which treat of the action of running water. It was from Lyell that Tennyson learned the significance of

> The sound of streams, that, swift or slow,
> Draw down Aeonian hills and sow
> The dust of continents to be.[1]

Lyell's book is permeated by a conception of which something has already been said at the beginning of this chapter, and which is of great importance in nineteenth century thought, the conception of universal Law. Lyell himself, who still believed in the permanent distinction of species, and would have nothing to do with any theory of development, explained the variation of species thus:

> We must suppose that when the Author of Nature creates an animal or plant, all the possible circumstances in which its descendants are destined to live are foreseen, and that an organisation is conferred upon it which will enable the species to perpetuate itself and survive under all varying circumstances to which it must inevitably be exposed.[2]

It takes many years before the conceptions of men like Lyell, Whewell and Herschel (already referred to), who are in the forefront of the thought of their time, filter down into the popular mind. In 1844 there appeared, anonymously, a book which was a popularisation of the advanced scientific thought of the previous forty years, *Vestiges of the Natural History of Creation*. This contained some old ideas, such as Lamarck's belief in the possibility of spontaneous generation, which were already out of date;

---

[1] *In Memoriam*, xxxv. Bradley (*Commentary*) points out that Tennyson probably derived this from 'works on geology'; the work was certainly Lyell's *Principles*. It may be remarked that in *In Memoriam* Tennyson did not definitely decide between the hypotheses of Cuvier and Lyell; any more than Milton in *Paradise Lost* decided between the Ptolemaic and Copernican systems.

[2] Vol. ii, pp. 23–4.

and it contained nothing new to scientists. At many points it anticipates *The Origin of Species*, still popularly believed to have been the earliest formulation of the theory of Evolution. But when it appeared, *Vestiges* was so new to the general public that it raised a storm; and went through twelve editions in a very short time. *Vestiges* is of very great interest to the student of the period, for it reveals the scientific thought which was then just at the stage of becoming public property, and was no longer confined to scientists and specialists. In the twelfth chapter there is a long passage which admirably sums up the position long held by advanced thinkers concerning the operation of law in nature, which was then beginning to become general; the substance of the author's views of organic creation is in these words:

> Let us seek in the history of the Earth's formation for a new suggestion at this point. We have seen powerful evidence that the construction of this globe and its associates, and inferentially all the other globes of space, was the result, not of any immediate or personal exertion on the part of the Deity, *but of natural laws which are the expression of His will.* What is to hinder our supposing that the organic creation is also the result of natural laws, which are in like manner an expression of His will?

In the last chapter of *Vestiges* the whole philosophical argument of the book is thus summarised:

> The Great Ruler of Nature has established laws for the operation of inanimate matter, which are quite unswerving, so that when we know them we have only to act in a certain way with respect to them in order to obtain all the benefits and avoid all the evils connected with them. He has likewise established moral laws in our nature, which are equally unswerving, and from obedience to which unfailing good is to be derived. But the two sets of laws are independent of each other. . . . It is clear, moreover, from the whole scope of the natural laws, that the individual, as far as the present sphere of being is concerned, is to the Author of Nature a consideration of inferior moment. Everywhere we see the arrangements for the species perfect; the individual is left, as it were, to take his chance amidst the mêlée of the various laws affecting him.

No student of Tennyson can read that passage without thinking of the famous section lv in *In Memoriam*

> Are God and Nature then at strife,
> That Nature lends such evil dreams?
> So careful of the type she seems,
> So careless of the single life.
>
> That I considering everywhere
> Her secret meaning in her deeds,
> And finding that of fifty seeds
> She often brings but one to bear,
>
> I falter where I firmly trod—

It is not suggested that the poem was indebted for this sentiment to the passage quoted from *Vestiges*; the idea was one of the leading preoccupations of all thinking men in the nineteenth century. Moreover, *In Memoriam* was contemporary with *Vestiges*, and the ideas to be seen in both were derived from common sources. But *Vestiges* at least supplies an independent expression, in prose, of much that Tennyson was expressing in *In Memoriam* during the late 'thirties and in the 'forties. A further, striking, example is to be seen in the section liv, which puts into most memorable language thoughts not unlike the final conclusion of *Vestiges*:

> It may be that, while we are committed to take our chance in the natural system of undeviating operation, and are left with apparent ruthlessness to endure the consequences of every collision into which we knowingly or unknowingly come with each law of the system, there is a system of Mercy and Grace behind the screen of nature, which is to make up for all the casualties endured here, and the very largeness of which is what makes these casualties a matter of indifference to God. For the existence of such a system, the actual constitution of nature is itself an argument.

Anyone doubting that the essence of true poetry lies, not in the thing said, but in the manner of its saying, would do well to compare that bald passage with the magnificent stanzas in which Tennyson expresses his dream:

> That nothing walks with aimless feet;
> That not one life shall be destroyed,
> Or cast as rubbish to the void
> When God hath made the pile complete.

The conception of universal law that had come in his youth to be held by thinkers who understood the conclusions of science, permeates Tennyson's poetry from end to end. It will suffice to give here only the most striking examples.

In the earliest of his notable philosophical poems, 'The Two Voices', which was written in the first darkness of his sorrow for Hallam, he thus describes the purpose of life which he had set himself to accomplish:

> As far as might be, to carve out
> Free space for every human doubt,
> That the whole mind might orb about.

> To search thro' all I felt or saw,
> The springs of life, the depths of awe,
> And reach the law within the law.

In 'The Higher Pantheism', he proclaims his acceptance of the legitimate conclusions of science, but decisively rejects the further conclusion, which came to be that of the scientific materialists of the later part of the nineteenth century:

> God is law, say the wise; O Soul, and let us rejoice,
> For if He thunder by law the thunder is yet His voice.

> Law is God, say some: no God at all, says the fool;
> For all we have power to see is a straight staff bent in a pool.

In *In Memoriam* as his uncontrollable grief begins to give place to a calmer mood, he recognises that the loss of his friend is part of the law that governs the Universe:

> I curse not nature, no, nor death;
> For nothing is that errs from law (lxxiii).

Towards the end of the poem, in recalling some occasion

associated with his friend,[1] he thinks of that time in terms of the identification of himself with the eternal law:

> Oh, wast thou with me, dearest, then,
> When I rose up against my doom,
> And yearned to burst the folded gloom,
> To bare the eternal Heavens again,
>
> To feel once more, in placid awe,
> The strong imagination roll
> A sphere of stars about my soul,
> In all her motion one with law:

In the lines to the Duke of Argyll, written in old age, he describes it as the highest achievement of human statesmanship to make

> This ever changing world of circumstance
> In changing, chime with never-changing law.

Most striking, perhaps, of all, are the lines in 'De Profundis' with which he greeted the birth of his son, Hallam, in August 1852:

> Out of the deep, my child, out of the deep
> *Thro' all this changing world of changeless law,*
> *And every phase of ever-heightening life,*
> And nine long months of antenatal gloom,
> With this last moon, this crescent—her dark orb
> Touched with earth's light—thou comest.[2]

The lines here italicised show, more clearly than any other passage in Tennyson's writings, how intimately his philosophical beliefs were based upon scientific knowledge; in this case upon biological knowledge. He reverts here to the fascinating conception, which he had already used more than twenty years earlier in 'The Palace of Art', of the progress of the human embryo through all the lower forms of life, which had been

---

[1] None of the commentators has identified the occasion, and Bradley points out the difficulty. But it does not affect the point here at issue.

[2] That there should be a reference to an astronomical phenomenon—that of 'the old moon in the new moon's arms'—in such a context is very characteristic.

revealed by embryologists in the first twenty years of the nineteenth century.[1] This was finally formulated by Haeckel, in the
dictum that the embryo, in its ontogeny, repeats its phylogeny.[2]
Put in less abstruse language, this means that every individual, in
its own development, exhibits a summary of the development of
the race. The early embryologists believed that the human
embryo was actually at one time a fish, at another a bird, and so on.
It is now known that the close resemblance is by no means identity.
The human infant, in the course of its inter-uterine life, never
actually is identical with an unborn puppy, close though the
resemblance can be. But this in no way detracts from the philosophical suggestiveness of the resemblance. Whether Tennyson,
who adopted the belief of the scientists of his youth, lived to
know the modern view does not matter. What matters is that he
was deeply affected by the implications of this glimpse of the
growing Tree of Life. The best known of his references to foetal
development—though it is safe to say that most readers have little
idea of what is meant—is to be found in the conclusion to *In
Memoriam*. Here, after describing the marriage of his sister
Cecilia to Lushington, the poet thinks of them on their honey-
moon; and then, in lines that rise far above the level of what has
just gone before, of the procreation of a new human being, that
shall climb the Tree of Life in its turn; and perhaps bring it
infinitesimally nearer to its fruition of perfected Humanity:

> A soul shall draw from out the vast
> And strike his being into bounds,
>
> And, moved thro' life of lower phase,
> Result in man, be born and think,
> And love and act, a closer link
> Betwixt us and the crowning race
>
> Of those that, eye to eye, shall look
> On knowledge; under whose command
> Is Earth and Earth's, and in their hand
> Is Nature like an open book;

---

[1] In the first edition of *Vestiges* (p. 198), there is an account of this idea. In the
second and later editions the passage is modified.
[2] *Generelle Morphologie der Organismen* (1866), vol. ii, p. 110 *seq.*

No longer half akin to brute,
For all we thought and loved and did
And hoped and suffered, is but seed
Of what in them is flower and fruit.

It is interesting to speculate whether this famous and beautiful passage owes anything to the first edition of *Vestiges*. We know that Tennyson asked for that book when it appeared, and said that it seemed to contain many ideas with which he had long been familiar.[1] His son asserted that the sections of *In Memoriam* which treat of Evolution had been read by Tennyson's friends before the publication of *Vestiges*, which is doubtless true of some, though not necessarily of all. *In Memoriam* was seventeen years in the writing, and Tennyson's friends, who had been shown portions of it as it progressed, would remember striking passages, such as those dealing with evolution; but they would certainly not remember, unless they had taken detailed notes, exactly which passages had been written by any particular year. Had any such notes survived, Hallam Tennyson would have known of them. We have seen that Tennyson had long been familiar with many of the matters popularised in *Vestiges*. The nebular hypothesis, some of the geology, and the idea of foetal development, all appear in poems written before 1844. It is, however, certain that the conclusion of *In Memoriam* was written not earlier than 1842, the date of the marriage of Cecilia Tennyson, and it may easily have been written later.[2] There is a very striking and suggestive resemblance between the expression 'the crowning race', and an expression in *Vestiges*; this is italicised in the following extract.[3]

It is startling to find an appearance of imperfection in the circle to which man belongs, and the ideas which rise in consequence are no less startling. *Is our race but the initial of the grand crowning type?* Are there yet to be species superior to us in organisation, purer in feeling, more powerful in device and act, and who shall take a rule over us?

[1] *Memoir*, vol. i, p. 223.
[2] This and other vexed points of chronology are discussed in Bradley's *Commentary*.
[3] *Vestiges*, p. 276. In the second and later editions the whole chapter in which this passage occurs is replaced by a much modified one containing nothing like this passage.

In *In Memoriam* it is assumed that 'the crowning race', of which Arthur Hallam seemed to Tennyson a type, would at least be of the human species, however far above the level of present humanity.—*Maud*, however, contains a remarkable passage which seems to be directly founded upon the passage in *Vestiges*. The lines in *Maud* at least prove that at some time before 1855 Tennyson had been strongly impressed by the idea that in the Cosmic Process, Man might be displaced by a higher species, as he had himself displaced the species which had preceded him:

> A monstrous eft was of old the Lord and Master of Earth,
> For him did the high sun flame and his river billowing ran,
> And he felt himself in his force to be nature's crowning race.
> As nine months go to the shaping an infant ripe for his birth,
> So many a million of ages have gone to the shaping of man.
> He now is first, but is he the last? Is he not too base?

That was written in the middle of a century which, by and large, and despite the increasing disillusionment of an ever-growing number of intelligent minds, believed in Progress. It had solid reason to. During the first half of the nineteenth century man's technological mastery of nature had made greater progress than had been achieved in all the, still uncounted, millennia of the existence of Homo Sapiens. And if, bearing in mind the discovery of the use of fire and the invention of the wheel (the dates of which are lost in the mists of time before man learnt to make records), that claim be denied to the mid-nineteenth century, it can hardly be denied to the mid-twentieth. After the two greatest wars of history, Homo Sapiens has now attained a mastery of physical nature which puts it within his power to destroy his species. That this power will never be unleashed, in some such conflict as one between the black and the white races, or between either of them and the yellow races, cannot now be confidently asserted. We have much more reason today than had Tennyson in 1855 for asking:

> He now is first, but is he the last? Is he not too base?

This passage from *Maud* contains once again, most significantly, the idea of foetal development; and it is stated in such a

E

way as to leave no doubt about the nature of Tennyson's interest in it. The analogy between the inter-uterine life of the human infant, and the 'many a million of ages' of terrestrial life that have gone to the development of Homo Sapiens, show most strikingly how the biological fact derived its fascination from its philosophical implications.

Great stress has been laid upon Tennyson's consciousness of the cruelty in Nature, as it is stated, for example, in *Maud*. The science of the nineteenth century shed upon natural processes a light more pitiless than had ever been shed before; and the effect upon a man so sensitive as Tennyson was profound, as may be seen from the famous sections lv and lvi of *In Memoriam*. Less than fifty years after Wordsworth proclaimed that 'Nature never did betray the heart that loved her', Tennyson, in a passage which has added a phrase to the English language, uttered this anguished cry about Nature:

> From scarped cliff and quarried stone
> She cries, 'A thousand types are gone:
> I care for nothing, all shall go.
>
> Thou makest thine appeal to me;
> I bring to life, I bring to death:
> The spirit does but mean the breath:
> I know no more.' And he, shall he,
>
> Man, her last work, who seemed so fair,
> Such splendid purpose in his eyes,
> Who rolled the psalm to wintry skies,
> Who built him fanes of fruitless prayer,
>
> Who trusted God was love indeed
> And love Creation's final law—
> Tho' Nature, red in tooth and claw
> With ravine, shriek'd against his creed—
>
> Who loved, who suffered countless ills,
> Who battled for the True, the Just,
> Be blown about the desert dust,
> Or seal'd within the iron hills?

No more? A monster then, a dream,
A discord. Dragons of the prime,
That tare each other in their slime,
Were mellow music matched with him.

But the true significance of Tennyson's debt to science will entirely escape us, if we consider this as the whole matter. It is only one half. If he was deeply sensitive to the implications of 'Nature red in tooth and claw', he was equally so to the implications of the fact that 'thro' lower lives I came'. The importance of the latter cannot be overestimated.

Tennyson looked courageously in the face of Nature, as he saw it with his very keen perception, and as it was revealed to him by the science of his age. He found in it cause both for joy and for despair. He expressed these in his poetry. But above all, and when he felt his vision to be widest and deepest, he found in Nature an inconceivably vast Cosmic Process according to Law, the evidence of some inscrutable, but unmistakable, Purpose. As he said near the end of In Memoriam (cxxviii):

I see in part
That all, as in some piece of art,
Is toil coöperant to an end.

This Cosmic Process had brought the solar system out of a gaseous nebula; it had produced the conditions which made possible organic life on Earth; it had led that life up from the lowest forms of organism, by a road still to be seen in the embryonic forms of Man. It had resulted in Man himself. Man still had within his own nature the taint of his ancestry, the traces of ape and tiger; if he proved unworthy of his sovereign place, it might yet produce a higher being to supersede him.

At this point in the argument, Tennyson looked within; for only there was it possible to find indications of the future; and only there might lie some solution to the enigma of the cruelty of the external world, and of Man's place in the Universe. The evidence supplied by his own nature was to Tennyson of the very highest importance, in his wrestling with the problems of Being and Reality. The famous section (cxxiv) of In Memoriam devoted to the intuition of Deity is not a very clear exposition, though the concluding lines are memorable:

Then was I as a child that cries,
But, crying, knows his father near;

And what I am beheld again
What is, and no man understands;
And out of darkness came the hands
That reach thro' nature, moulding men[1]

A better exposition of his fundamental position is to be found in
'The Two Voices'; it should be remembered that this was written
when Tennyson had not long come to manhood, and it does not
contain the whole solution which he reached later; but nowhere is
there more clearly revealed the mind of its author than in these
remarkable stanzas. The Voice, after failing to persuade him
to kill himself, dwells upon death; but he replies that the evidence
of the senses may not be conclusive as to the destiny of Man:

Who forged that other influence,
That heat of inward evidence,
By which he doubts against the sense?

He owns the fatal gift of eyes,
That read his spirit blindly wise,
Not simple as a thing that dies.

Here sits he shaping wings to fly;
His heart forebodes a mystery;
He names the name Eternity.

That type of Perfect in his mind
In Nature can he nowhere find.
He sows himself on every wind.

He seems to hear a Heavenly Friend,
And thro' thick veils to apprehend
A labour working to an end.

[1] Bradley's *Commentary* on this section runs (p. 228): 'In this great poem he still
thinks of the spiritual conflict of the past. "That Nameless to which we call, divined
everywhere but not to be understood, where did I find him? Not in evidence drawn
from Nature, nor in questions which the intellect raises and seeks to answer; but
when the heart felt and cried upon him like a child I beheld him, and saw that
through Nature he moulds man".'

The end and the beginning vex
His reason; many things perplex,
With motions, checks and counterchecks.

He knows a baseness in his blood
At such strange war with something good,
He may not do the thing he would.

Heaven opens inward, chasms yawn,
Vast images in glimmering dawn,
Half shown, are broken and withdrawn.

The doubt, the difficulty, and the intuition expressed in that
magnificent passage remained with Tennyson always; but the
doubt grew less and less; and the intuition grew stronger. The
same debate between doubt and intuition—perhaps between the
two sides of Tennyson's own nature—is the subject of a poem of
his old age, 'The Ancient Sage'. At the end, the Sage tells the
youth how it is possible to see, beyond the range of Night and
Shadow,

The high-heaven dawn of more than mortal day
Strike on the mount of vision—

Tennyson himself saw that dawn.

It seemed to him in his maturity that the Process visible in
external Nature, which had produced Man, was also taking place
in the moral nature of Man himself. For the race it might in
some far future result in a perfected Humanity. For the individual
it could assuredly result in a conquest of the lower nature; in a
surrender of the individual will to the furtherance of that Purpose
behind the Process which such conquest seemed to reveal:

Our wills are ours, we know not how;
Our wills are ours to make them thine.

It should be noted in passing that the 'argument from intuition',
so consistently advanced by Tennyson for his belief in the
beneficence of the Purpose which he called God, is not primarily
an emotional matter, and the dismissal of it as 'wishful thinking'

is an unintelligent comment. Because 'wishful thinking' means an attempt to rationalise emotions which have in fact no rational basis. Had Tennyson merely done that—and *In Memoriam* contains the history of his temptation to do it—it would have led him to the conclusion to which it led Thomas Hardy: that the Universe is a ghastly business, and that 'it is just the same in everything. Nothing was made for man'.[1] Tennyson's argument is primarily a rational one, based upon analogy; the analogy is with the evolutionary process in nature, the conception of which is certainly among the greatest achievements of the human reason. As far as reason would take him, Tennyson (intensely emotional though he was) went with reason. Even the further step, which was by intuition, was not without rational sanction.

Both Tennyson's masterpieces, *In Memoriam* and *Maud*, have as their real subject the spiritual evolutionary process in the life of an individual. From the nature of that process in his own heart, Tennyson, when at his highest and serenest, believed what he could not prove: that the Purpose behind the Process, both in the physical and moral worlds, was good—that it was the God

> Who ever lives and loves.

And finally, the supreme implication of the evolutionary process was an intimation of the continuance of the individual life beyond death:

> Eternal process moving on,
> From state to state the spirit walks;
> And these are but the shattered stalks,
> Or ruined chrysalis of one (lxxxii).

After what has been said, it is hardly necessary to illustrate this doctrine of the Process in greater detail from the whole corpus of Tennyson's poetry. It will suffice to take only the most personal of them, *In Memoriam*:

At the beginning, when he is in the darkest hours of his cruel fellowship with Sorrow, the process of Nature seems to him empty, useless and meaningless (section iii). In section xxxv, the

---

[1] *Two on a Tower*, ch. 4. The matter is discussed in detail in ch. 3 of my *Thomas Hardy: A Study of his Writings and their Background*. (Basil Blackwell, Oxford 1938; reprinted by Russell and Russell, New York, 1962).

endless process which makes continents is again described as meaningless to human love, for whom it is identified with the process of the corruption of the body in death. In the famous sections lv and lvi there is a closer analysis of process in nature. Apparently, at this point in the poem, it appears as largely waste; and raises the question: shall Man, the culmination of it, be himself of no account, and blown as dust about the desert? In section cxviii comes the answer which Tennyson gives to his own earlier doubts and agonies. Contemplate the process, runs this answer, and do not think of human love and death only in terms of organic nature, but in terms of an analogy between organic and spiritual processes. As biological organic process has, 'thro' cyclic storms', given rise to Man, who is the highest type of being known to us, and the herald of a race higher than himself, so in like manner the spiritual evolution within Man's moral nature suggests, for the individual, a 'higher place' beyond the fetters of matter, provided that he remains true, while still within those fetters, to the Purpose behind the Process. In section cxx this theme is continued on a purely personal plane. Tennyson here in retrospect says: 'It is not in vain that I have fought with death, because I have discovered that we are not only cunning casts in clay. If science proves us to be so, science is useless to mankind and to me; and I do not wish to live to see it'.[1] In section cxxiii he returns, in the mood of tranquillity to which he has now attained, to the thought of the eternal geological changes of the Earth which had, at the beginning, given him such anguish. Bradley, in connection with this section, most aptly quotes the beautiful lines from the 'Ode on the Death of the Duke of Wellington':

> For though the Giant Ages heave the hill
> And break the shore, and evermore
> Make and break, and work their will;
> Though world on world in myriad myriads roll

[1] The very difficult last quatrain, which nobody has yet elucidated satisfactorily, does not affect the question. Bradley is probably right in suggesting that it contains a reference to Tennyson's belief concerning the pre-existence of the soul; there are many traces of the doctrine of Anamnesis in Tennyson; but it is not an explanation of the real difficulty. I would suggest the following interpretation: 'The science of the future may teach man to act from childhood like the greater ape; in my time it was not so, for I was born to a better heritage'. This would foreshadow Tennyson's later views of the abuse of science.

Round us, each with different powers,
And other forms of life than ours,
What know we greater than the soul?

In the conclusion (which is really an epilogue) to *In Memoriam* occurs the passage already quoted, in which the thought of the procreation of a new human being leads to a mental recapitulation of the whole evolutionary process; a process finally to culminate in the divine consummation of the Universe.

Such, then, is the debt which Tennyson owes to the science of the nineteenth century. It is a debt greater than any poet has ever owed to science, greater than the debt of Dante or Milton, or even Goethe. For the troubled twentieth century it has a double message. The first is that all knowledge is the legitimate province of the poet capable of creative thought. The second is a personal one. We live today under the shadow of the possible destruction of humanity. Tennyson lived in an age of political peace, but of intense spiritual warfare; and from the death wounds given in that conflict many of the troubles of our time arise. Tennyson had himself been through that conflict; and, having escaped the death of the spirit, he ceased to fear so greatly the death of the body and the inevitable destruction of the material, terrestrial tenement of the soul. For he knew this to be but a part of the Cosmic Process; beyond the full understanding of man, indeed, but not beyond the control of the Purpose behind the Universe:

Will my tiny spark of being wholly vanish in your deeps and heights?
Must my day be dark by reason, O ye Heavens, of your boundless
    nights,
Rush of suns, and roll of systems, and your fiery clash of meteorites?

'Spirit, nearing yon dark portal at the limit of thy human state,
Fear not thou the hidden purpose of that Power which alone is great,
Nor the myriad world, His shadow, nor the silent Opener of the Gate.'

CHAPTER THREE

THE 'RELIGIONS OF HUMANITY'

Having done their utmost to abolish a thousand years of history, it is not surprising that the French Revolutionaries proceeded to 'abolish' God. This event, which has some claim to be the moral nadir of the whole revolution, took place on 10th November, 1793, and was called 'La Fête de la Raison'. For the sake of his inimitable style, two paragraphs may be quoted from Carlyle's account:[1]

Out of which strange fall of Formulas, tumbling there in confused welter, betrampled by the Patriotic dance (La Carmagnole), is it not passing strange to see a *new* Formula arise? For the human tongue is not adequate to speak what 'triviality run distracted' there is in human nature. Black Mumbo-Jumbo of the woods, and most Indian Wau-Waus, one can understand; but this of Procureur *Anaxagoras*, whilom John Peter, Chaumette? We will say only: Man is a born idol worshipper, *sight*-worshipper, so sensuous-imaginative is he; and also partakes much of the nature of an ape.

For the same day, while this brave Carmagnole-dance has hardly jigged itself out, there arrive Procureur Chaumette and Municipals and Departmentals, and with them the strangest freightage: a New Religion! Demoiselle Candeille, of the Opera; a woman fair to look upon, when well rouged; she, borne on palanquin shoulder-high, with red woollen nightcap; an azure mantle; garlanded with oak, holding in her hand the Pike of Jupiter-*Peuple*, sails in; heralded by white young women girt in tricolor. Let the world consider it! This, O National Convention, wonder of the Universe, is our new Divinity: *Goddess of Reason*, worthy, and alone worthy of revering. Her henceforth we adore. Nay, were it too much to ask of an august National Representation that it also went with us to the *ci-devant* Cathedral called of Notre Dame, and executed a few strophes in worship of her?

[1] *The French Revolution*, vol. 3, bk. V, ch. I.

The reign of the Goddess of Reason was not a long one. Barely seven months later, on 8th June, 1794, the Hébertists, Danton and Demoulins having all gone to the guillotine, Robespierre, himself only a few weeks from his fall on Thermidor 9 (i.e. July 27), inaugurated a new religion. Carlyle again may be quoted:[1]

> On the day they call *Décadi*, New Sabbath, 20 Prairial, 8th June by old style, what thing is this going forward in the Jardin National, whilom Tuileries Garden? All the world is there in holiday clothes. . . . This day, if it please Heaven, we are to have, on improved Anti-Chaumette principles: a New Religion.
> Catholicism being burned out, and Reason-worship guillotined, was there not need of one? Incorruptible Robespierre, not unlike the Ancients, as legislator of a free people, will now be Priest and Prophet. He has donned his sky-blue coat, made for the occasion; white silk waistcoat broidered with silver, black silk breeches, white stockings, shoe-buckles of gold. He is President of the Convention; he has made the Convention *decree*, so they name it, *décréter*, the 'Existence of the Supreme Being', and likewise '*ce principe consolateur*' of the Immortality of the Soul. These consolatory principles, the basis of rational Republican Religion, are getting decreed; and here, on this blessed *Décadi*, by help of Heaven and Painter David, is to be our first act of worship.
> (Carlyle then describes the proceedings, which culminate in setting fire to 'hideous statues of Atheism, Anarchy and such like, (which) thanks to Heaven and Painter David strike abhorrence into the heart'; and continues):
> And then? Why, then, there is other Processioning, scraggy Discoursing, and—this is our Feast of the Etre Suprème; our new Religion, better or worse, is come!—Look at it one moment, O Reader, not two. The shabbiest page of Human Annals: or is there, that thou wottest of, one shabbier? Mumbo-Jumbo of the African woods to me seems venerable beside this new Deity of Robespierre; for this is a *conscious* Mumbo-Jumbo, and *knows* that he is machinery. O sea-green Prophet, unhappiest of wind-bags blown nigh to bursting, what distracted Chimera among realities art thou growing to!

However deplorable and contemptible they look at this

[1] Ibid, Bk. VI, ch. 4.

distance, the throes of the French Revolution were the birth-pangs of the modern world. One offspring of that womb grew to considerable stature during the nineteenth century, and exerted, for a time, much influence. This was the so-called 'Positive Philosophy', and its subsequent elaborations, of Auguste Comte; which he himself regarded as the ultimate constructive Synthesis to emerge out of the transitional chaos resulting from the collapse of unscientific modes of thought, of which the French Revolution was the typical example. The whole basis of Comte's system is to be found in what he claimed to be the fundamental law of human development, discovered by himself, 'La Loi des Trois Etats'. John Morley described this as follows:

> Each of our leading conceptions, each branch of our knowledge, passes successively through three different phases; there are three different ways in which the human mind explains phenomena, each way following the other in order. These three stages are the theological, the metaphysical and the positive. Knowledge, or a branch of knowledge, is in the theological state when it supposes the phenomena under consideration to be due to immediate volition, either in the object or in some supernatural being. In the metaphysical state, for volition is substituted abstract force residing in the object, yet existing independently of the object; the phenomena are viewed as if apart from the bodies manifesting them; and the properties of each substance have attributed to them an existence distinct from that substance. In the positive state inherent volition or external volition and inherent force or abstraction personified have both disappeared from men's minds, and the explanation of a phenomenon means a reference of it, by way of succession or resemblance, to some other phenomenon—means the establishment of a relation between the given fact and some more general fact. In the theological and metaphysical states, men seek a cause or an essence; in the positive they are content with a law.[1]

Applying these conceptions to the evolution of human society, Comte reached the conclusion that the Positive stage of history results in the realisation that Humanity, past, present and to come, is 'Le Grand Etre':

[1] Auguste Comte (he had four more Christian names) 1798–1857. His chief, but not only, works are: *Cours de philosophie positive* (1830–42); *Système de politique positive* (1852–4); *Catéchisme positive* (1852). Morley's words, which refer to the first work, are from his article in the *Encyclopedia Britannica*.

A deeper study of the great universal order reveals to us at length the ruling power within it of the true Great Being, whose destiny it is to bring that order continually to perfection by constantly conforming to its laws, and which thus best represents to us that system as a whole. This undeniable Providence, the supreme dispenser of our destinies, becomes in the natural course the common centre of our affections, our thoughts and our actions. Although this Great Being evidently exceeds the utmost strength of any, even of any collective, human force, its necessary constitution and its peculiar function endow it with the truest sympathy towards all its servants. The least among us can and ought constantly to aspire to maintain and even to improve this Being.[1]

This 'Religion of Humanity' is expounded in its greatest detail in the *Catechism of Positive Religion*:

But (asks the Lady of the Priest in the Catechism) does the Positive Religion, perhaps, puff up the intellect and dry up the heart? No, my daughter, the Priest (Comte) replies; on the contrary, it appeals to the heart through *the great conception of Humanity*, or the *Great Being*. By this grand idea 'The conception of God will be entirely superseded'; here at last is the true object of worship, recognizable as real; yet demanding as much reverence and devoted service as any theological fiction.

Hitherto men have worshipped imaginary beings, vainly endeavouring 'to see without them what had no existence but within'. Positivism, on the other hand, offers a new Divinity which, instead of subsisting in 'solemn inaction', like the old Supreme Being, is alive and present and dynamic, and which, moreover, depends for its very existence upon the *love* of its worshippers. 'Humanity' differs from all previous gods in its very need of our service, in the pathos of its appeal to us to preserve it and make it more god-like; in the Positive Religion alone, 'the object of worship is a Being whose nature is relative, modifiable and perfectible'. It is in this way that by the new worship we are at the same time producing Progress, which is 'the development of Order under the influence of Love'.

The foregoing is a quotation from the chapter on Comte in

[1] From the composite English translation by Bridges and others (1875–9) of the *Politique*. All Comte's major works were translated into English by 1880, and had a considerable vogue; largely because of the interest of J. S. Mill, Herbert Spencer, T. H. Huxley and others.

Professor Basil Willey's *Nineteenth Century Studies* (1949), which is perhaps the best short account of the subject in English. It is not only a brilliant synopsis of Comte's ideas, but also, in the preceding and following chapters, Willey gives an authoritative and illuminating account of their influence upon other writers, notably John Stuart Mill and George Eliot. He describes how G. H. Lewes (George Eliot's husband in all but name), acclaimed the Positive Philosophy as 'the dawn of a new era'; and goes on, not unnaturally, to ask:

> Why then has the Comtean sun been so soon and so thoroughly eclipsed? A number of causes might be suggested; the verbosity and boring redundancy of his works, his conceit, his excessive love of 'system'—leading in his later phases to something like monomania, and his reactionary propensities, which antagonised his own admirers. Above all, he was eclipsed by Marx, who also spoke as one having authority, and whose doctrines, unlike Comte's, could serve immediately as the platform of a political party. Comte was a far more comprehensive thinker than Marx, but he left unanswered the great immediate question 'where do we go from *here*?' and so his colossal effort proved an Icarus-flight.[1]

At the end of the chapter, Willey makes this criticism of Comte:

> He moved inexorably along mental tramlines, and so could never deviate from his own groove enough to ask the fundamental, the damaging questions: *can* science be itself a philosophy? *can* we dispense with metaphysical enquiry? *can* we go on worshipping ourselves?[2]

The twentieth century has answered at least two of these questions. Science *cannot* be itself a philosophy. We know now that that was one of the delusions of the nineteenth century. Nearly a generation ago, Sir James Jeans (in *The Mysterious Universe*) was already saying that, so far from making any further dogmatic pronouncements, it was time that scientists should stop making them. And in his *The Individual and the Universe* (Reith Lectures 1958), Sir Bernard Lovell speaks in these terms:

[1] Op. cit. p. 187.
[2] Ibid., p. 202.

On the question of the validity of combining a metaphysical
and physical process as a description of creation, this, as I said
earlier, is the individual's problem. . . . I am certainly not
competent to discuss this problem of knowledge outside that
acquired by my scientific tools, and my outlook is essentially a
simple one. Simple in the sense that I am no more surprised
or distressed at the limitation of science when faced with this
great problem of creation than I am at the limitation of the
spectroscope in describing the radiance of a sunset or at the
theory of counterpoint in describing the beauty of a fugue.[1]

As to the third of the fundamental questions which Comte left
unanswered: the two world wars of the first half of the twentieth
century, to say nothing of their aftermath and what it has revealed
of human nature, have finally removed the possibility of worship-
ping ourselves.

Today, not much more than a century after it was launched,
Comte's 'Religion of Humanity' has finally sunk, almost without
a trace. At most, perhaps, there is left floating among the ever
increasing jetsam of jargon from obsolescent and obsolete ideas
the phrase 'logical positivism'. Once it was a ringing battle cry;
but now we are reaching the stage when the younger generations,
coming across it, reach for their dictionaries. As a battle cry, it
has been replaced by another phrase, also coined in the nineteenth
century, 'dialectical materialism'. If there is a new religion in the
twentieth century which has really moved the minds and hearts
of men, and had a profound influence in human society, it is the
one of which Marx and Engels were the founders. To say that the
new religion of the twentieth century has proved to be Commun-
ism is probably true. But to say it is also to use the word 'religion'
in a new sense, the discussion of which would be beyond the
scope of these pages. Did not the Founding Father of Com-
munism himself describe religion as 'the opium of the people'?

The essential central tenet of the 'new religion' proclaimed by
Comte is to be found in an English poet, of whom, at first sight,
it might be least expected—Swinburne. Unlike the other major
creative writer of the period in England to be influenced by
'Positivism', George Eliot, Swinburne is most unlikely to have
read any Comte. I know of no evidence that he did; and neither
social—or any other—science, nor contemporary philosophy ever

[1] P. 110.

interested him. But the conception of a 'Religion of Humanity', not necessarily Comtean in its details, had by 1870 become part of the intellectual climate of opinion. It was in that year that Swinburne wrote:

Not each man of all men is God, but God is the fruit of the whole.

In England, Swinburne has been out of fashion for forty years.[1] Only one English scholar, as far as I know, has during that period devoted any attention to him (which must shortly be considered). Indeed, that part of Swinburne's poetry containing the poem from which this line is taken has never had proper attention paid to it. Everybody knows, or at least knew a generation ago:

When the hounds of Spring are on Winter's traces—

and:

Thou hast conquered, O pale Galilean; the world has grown grey from thy breath—.

Atalanta in Calydon and *Poems and Ballads* were (despite T. S. Eliot and his disciples) classics. In that sense, *Songs before Sunrise* has never been a classic and is never likely to become one. And yet it contains at least as good poetry as he ever wrote before, and much better than any—with one or two exceptions—he ever wrote after. It contains, indeed, some of the most beautiful poetry in the English language. If that claim seems startling, the reason is easy to give; for it is also some of the most difficult—not intellectually, but psychologically. The line just quoted is fairly well known. So is the last line of the same poem, the 'Hymn of Man', written during the Vatican Council of 1870 (which promulgated the dogma of Papal Infallibility) and as a counterblast to it:

Glory to Man in the highest! for Man is the master of things.

So, possibly, is the simplest stanza of a far from simple poem:

---

[1] The United States, however, has made notable contributions to Swinburne studies, the greatest being Prof. C. Y. Lang's magnificent 6 vol. edition of the Letters (1959–62).

A creed is a rod,
　　And a crown is of night;
　But this thing is God,
　　To be man with thy might,
To grow straight in the strength of thy spirit, and live out thy life as
　　the light. ('Hertha').

But what about the following:

Men that forsook thee hast thou not forsaken,
　　Races of men that knew not hast thou known;
Nations that slept thou hast doubted not to waken,
　　Worshippers of strange Gods to make thine own.

All old grey histories hiding thy clear features,
　　O secret spirit and sovereign, all men's tales,
Creeds woven of men thy children and thy creatures,
　　They have woven for vestures of thee and for veils.

Thine hands, without election or exemption,
　　Feed all men fainting from false peace or strife,
O thou, the resurrection and redemption,
　　The godhead and the manhood and the life.
　　　　　　　　　　　　　　　　　('Mater Triumphalis').

That, unmistakably, is the language of religion. But what
religion, and to whom is it addressed? And what of this?:

Am I not he that hath made thee and begotten thee,
　　I, God, the spirit of Man?
Wherefore now these eighteen years hast thou forgotten me,
　　From whom thy life began?

——————

I am Freedom, God and man, O France, that plead with thee;
　　How long now shall I plead?
Was I not with thee in travail, and in need with thee,
　　Thy sore travail and need?
Thou wast fairest and first of my virgin-vested daughters,
　　Fairest and foremost thou;
And thy breast was white, though thy hands were red with slaughters,
　　Thy breast, a harlot's now. ('Quia Multum Amavit')

That, whether you choose to call it the language of religion or not, is unquestionably the language of the Authorised Version of the Bible.

We are a long way, here, from the dry and dogmatic ratiocination of Auguste Comte. This was not the kind of language that the priest used to his 'daughter' in the Catechism of Positive Religion (it might well be said that there is no doubt which of them is the most 'positive' in the ordinary English sense of the word!) Nevertheless, this is the authentic Religion of Humanity, as Swinburne conceived it; and, one is constrained to say in passing, it is very much more human, and much more genuinely religious, too, than anything in Comte. The difficulty for us, in imaginatively apprehending it and responding to it, is of two kinds. The first is that Swinburne's Religion of Humanity is expounded in *Songs before Sunrise* in terms of a contemporary political situation which, for us, has no universal significance, and indeed hardly any meaning at all. The tremendous lines from 'Quia Multum Amavit' are addressed to the France of 1870. They are concerned with Napoleon III and the Franco-Prussian war. To us, a hundred years later, who remember 1914 and 1940, all that is nothing. Much the same is true of the poems concerned with Italy. Mazzini, Garibaldi and the Risorgimento created the Italian nation. Since then, it has had a hundred years of history, which included Fascism, Mussolini and the second world war.

A further consideration enters into the 'unreality' of Swinburne's position. How much objective reality did it have, even in 1868–70? He was a good French scholar on paper;[1] and he at least read, and to some extent wrote, Italian. How well he spoke either language there is hardly any evidence. But he never lived in either country, and knew neither of them at first hand. Italy he only visited twice in his life, for a few weeks as a tourist. He did not even have long or regular intercourse with any expatriate French or Italian community in England (notwithstanding his intercourse of some months with Mazzini). His violent emotions towards both countries had practically no basis outside himself. Few men are so made. Had he known the language, read its literature, visited it once for a month and consorted with one political exile from it, he might have developed just such an

---

[1] He went too far, as Mallarmé testified, in thinking he could write French poetry.

F

emotion for Afghanistan (threatened, he would have said, by Britain from the south and Russia from the north). The whole thing was almost entirely subjective. Our emotions do not share it; and that is why it puzzles us. To us, the France of 1870 is not and cannot be 'a harlot' of 18 years standing. And many of us, who know France as Swinburne never knew her, and have seen such things as the symbolic broken sword on the memorial to Jean Moulin at Chartres, love her no less than he. No poet can be expected to anticipate the political emotions of a century after his day. But, if they are founded upon the realities of his own day, his political emotions have some chance of being understood by posterity. Even as we, after a longer interval, understand

> Bliss was it in that dawn to be alive

and

> Men are we and must grieve when even the shade
> Of that which once was great has passed away.

A further difficulty with *Songs before Sunrise* is frequent in another form of unreality than the psychological. This is best illustrated by an example from one of the finest of them, 'Tiresias'. Writing to George Powell on 17th April 1868,[1] Swinburne said:

> I have such a subject before me untouched—Tiresias at the grave of Antigone—i.e. (understand) Dante at the grave of Italia. I do not say the living heir of Dante as a patriot, for *he* sees her slowly but hopefully rising, though with pain and shame and labour.

The poem is divided into two parts; the first part, consisting of 43 stanzas

> 'is put into the mouth of the great Theban seer, who appears several times in Greek poetry but whose name is probably familiar to us from the part which he plays in the *Oedipus Rex* and the *Antigone*'.[2]

---

[1] Lang, No. 260.
[2] W. R. Rutland: *Swinburne: A Nineteenth Century Hellene* (Basil Blackwell, Oxford 1931), p. 300 et seq.; in which the first part of the poem is discussed at length.

This first part is in itself a magnificent poem, though its full appreciation demands considerable classical scholarship (like so many great English poems). But the second part, describing the resurrection of a dead woman from a grave by three prophets, is hardly intelligible. The identity of the woman is revealed by the last line.

Are these dead, or art thou dead, Italy?

That the first prophet is Dante is clear from several allusions. But without knowledge of Swinburne's biography, nobody could identify the 'Third Prophet' as Mazzini. The identity of the second prophet is problematic.[1] The language is, indeed, superb. Italy is resurrected by faith

> Faith above creeds, faith beyond records, born
> Of the pure, naked, fruitful, awful morn.

Such faith Swinburne, no doubt largely under the influence of Mazzini, had at that time created within himself. It was faith of an authentically religious nature, such as is described in the *Epistle to the Hebrews:* 'Faith is the substance of things hoped for, the evidence of things not seen.' The writer of that Epistle goes on to give examples of it from history, and it is here that Swinburne seems to fail us, because we do not think of there ever having been, in history, a free and united Italy; and her resurrection, therefore, is to us an anachronism. But here Swinburne was entirely true to his Italian contemporaries. To them, the Italy which would rise from the Risorgimento (the 'rising again') would be 'la terza Italia', the third Italy—the first having been Rome, and the second the Italy of the Renaissance. This is

---

[1] The most probable identification seems to be Michelangelo. But Swinburne himself seems to have been by no means certain. Writing to Michael Rossetti on 28th August 1870, he said:

I am writing a poem on Tiresias at the grave of Antigone—the living buried woman representing liberty in the abstract (or more especially as incarnate in Italy—but I always identify the two as it were, in this book) during the years 'while the Earth cried, where art thou?' And the prophet, any patriot or free thinker you will, from Dante to Mazzini; but it is difficult clearly and comprehensibly to combine without confusing the type and the antitype, especially as the Theban story with its infinite suggestions and significances fairly carries me away like a wave, forgetful for the time of symbol and modern application. (Lang, 363).

The description of Dante as a 'freethinker' does not help towards our comprehension.

perfectly illustrated by the Sonnet which Carducci addressed to Mazzini in 1872.[1] As for Dante, the sixth centenary of his birth had fallen in 1865. And to such men as Mazzini and Carducci, he appeared almost as the very Angel of the Resurrection of Italy. His spirit seemed to appear bodily before them and say 'She is not dead'. Here is the beginning of the first of the three Sonnets which Carducci wrote about Dante in May 1865:

> Io 'l vidi. Su l'avello iscoverchiato
> Erto l'imperial vate levosse:
> Allor la sua Marina Adria commosse,
> E tremò de l'Italia il manco lato.[2]

The Religion of Humanity which Swinburne professes and proclaims in *Songs before Sunrise* presents us with another difficulty: the variety and multiplicity of the names given to its Deity. In the 'Hymn of Man', where this is deliberately contrasted with the God of the priests of Rome (and very occasionally elsewhere in the book), it is simply 'Man'. Since it is laid down that

Not each man of all men is God, but God is the fruit of the whole

we are quite prepared for the corollary

Glory to Man in the highest, for Man is the master of things¡

More commonly, however, it is some emotion or abstract quality personified, with or without additions, the significance of which is difficult of analysis, and still more difficult of definition; e.g.

[1] Da quelli scogli, onde Colombo infante
Nuovi pe 'l mar vedea mondi spuntare,
Egli vide nel ciel crepuscolare
Co 'l cuor di Gracco ed il pensier di Dante
La terza Italia; e con le luci fise
A lei trasse per mezzo un cimitero,
E un popol morto dietro a lui si mise. . . .

From those cliffs, whence the child Colombus saw new worlds rise in the sea, he saw in the twilight sky with the heart of Gracchus and the thought of Dante, the third Italy; and with steadfast eyes he drew a cemetery across her, and a dead people placed themselves behind him.

[2] I saw him. Upon the uncovered tomb the imperial prophet rose erect: then Adria shook its coast and the left side of Italy trembled. The Dante sonnets are in *Levia Gravia*, the Mazzini sonnet in *Giambi ed Epodi*. Gosse (*Life of Swinburne*, p. 192) says that Swinburne was, and remained, unaware of the existence of Carducci.

O soul, O God, O glory of Liberty. . . .

('Eve of Revolution')

or

Love, the belovèd Republic . . . .

('Hertha')

In passing, it may be remarked that the realism of these phrases is not increased by our consciousness that the united Italy which finally did emerge was not a republic, but a monarchy. And in 1868–70 France was not a republic either; which is of course why Swinburne called her 'harlot'. But much the commonest form of his Humanity-Divinity is a female one. It is 'Mater Dolorosa'. It is 'Mater Triumphalis'. It is a whole variety of what modern psychological jargon calls a 'mother figure'. Most notably of all, it is Hertha-Yggdrasil. To this very original and remarkable poem we must now turn. Here, if anywhere, we have the essential Creed of his Religion of Humanity.

In one of the most interesting of all his letters[1] Swinburne gives an account of the development of his own religious convictions, which culminates in this passage:

> (But) we who worship no material incarnation of any qualities, no person, may worship the divine (man) humanity, the ideal of human perfection and aspiration, without worshipping any God, any person, any fetish at all. Therefore I might call myself if I wished a kind of Christian—that is, taking the semi-legendary Christ as type of human aspiration and perfection, and supposing (if you like) that Jesus may have been the highest and purest sample of man on record—of the church of Blake and Shelley, but assuredly no Theist.

Later in the same letter he says:

> Of all I have done I rate *Hertha* highest as a single piece, finding in it the most lyric force and music combined with the most of condensed and clarified thought. I think there really is a good deal compressed and concentrated into that poem.

In his *Life of Swinburne*,[2] Edmund Gosse wrote:

---

[1] Dated 20th February, 1875. Lang, No. 600.

[2] First published in 1917—the indispensable foundation of all Swinburne scholarship, despite all that has appeared (even from the same pen) since. My quotation is from pp. 194–5.

Swinburne's claim to be considered as among the most
purely philosophical of all the English poets is founded on
several numbers of *Songs before Sunrise*, none of which are
directly occupied with the aims of Mazzini or the errors of
Napoleon III. In 'Mater Triumphalis', in the 'Prelude' and the
'Epilogue', in 'The Litany of Nations', in 'Hertha' pre-
eminently, we see a statement of Swinburne's loftiest doctrine.
. . . The emotion of the poet in presence of the supreme and
eternal characteristics of the Universe gave to the noblest parts
of *Songs before Sunrise* an intensity unique in English literature,
and probably to be compared with nothing else written since
the Greeks produced cosmological hymns in the fifth century
B.C.

However that may be—and the deliberate panegyric is worth
quoting—'Hertha' is, beyond contradiction, one of Swinburne's
most original and powerful achievements. In his interesting essay
on it, of which more must be said later, E. M. W. Tillyard writes
of 'Hertha':

'I know no Victorian poem of comparable length that catches
up so much contemporary and anticipates so much modern
thought.'[1] The name 'Hertha' (cognate with our 'hearth') comes
from Tacitus as that of a goddess of the Germanic tribes. The
poem is, indeed, put into the mouth of a female divinity:

> I am that which began;
>   Out of me the years roll;
>   Out of me God and man;
>   I am equal and whole;
> God changes, and man, and the form of them bodily; I am the soul.

> Before ever land was,
>   Before ever the sea,
>   Or soft hair of the grass,
>   Or fair limb so of the tree,
> Or the flesh-coloured fruit of my branches, I was, and thy soul was in
> me.

Already the reader familiar only with classical goddesses is in
difficulty. What is 'the flesh-coloured fruit of my branches'—
and what sort of a goddess has branches? The answer is simple,

---

[1] E. M. W. Tillyard: *Five Poems* (1948), p. 87.

and curious. As far as I know, this is the only place in all his voluminous writings in which Swinburne is referring, not to Mediterranean, but to Germanic, sources. He knew not one word of German, or its literature, and was rather proud of his ignorance. But his source here is Icelandic, or (to give it the proper technical name) Old Norse. In Scandinavian mythology, Yggdrasil was the mystical ash tree which symbolised existence; it was at once the tree of life, of knowledge, of space and of time. Its roots went down into the realms of death; its stem upheld the world; its top reached above the heavens. Under its branches, at the summit of the rainbow, sat the three Fates ('Norns'); whose names in Old Norse signified the Past, the Present and the Future.[1] Since all Germanic literature, past or present, was, with this single exception, *terra incognita* to Swinburne, it is interesting to speculate where he learnt about Yggdrasil. William Morris, who translated the Volsunga Saga, was of course a great friend. Perhaps a more likely source was George Powell, to whom Swinburne wrote on 25th November 1865, thanking him for the First Series of his *Legends of Iceland*, published the previous year.[2]

There is one other, not insignificant, detail in 'Hertha' which Swinburne got from the same source. Here are stanzas 36 and 37:

> Lo, winged with world's wonders,
> With miracles shod,
> With fires of his thunders
> For raiment and rod,

[1] Urthr, Verthandi and Skuld; the words are cognates of parts of the verb 'to be' (the second being the modern High German 'werdend', which Goethe, it will be remembered, uses in its substantival form in *Faust*).

[2] The frontispiece to this volume is a stylised representation of Yggdrasil; although no allusion to Yggdrasil is to be found in it; or in the sequel, entitled Second Series, published in 1866. This latter, however, is dedicated to Lord Dufferin and Swinburne; and the introductory essay with which it opens contains a quotation from Atalanta. At this time, Swinburne made the acquaintance of the Icelandic scholar who had collaborated with Powell, G. Vigfusson; see Lang, Nos. 88 and 89. Powell and Vigfusson were to produce a notable edition, with translations, of much of Old Norse poetry in 1883: *Corpus Poeticum Boreale*, Oxford, 2 vols. This contains the text of at least one poem alluding to Yggdrasil; which Swinburne must have been shown and had explained to him by 1868; because two lines in 'Hertha' contain a translation of two of the Old Norse lines:

> Though sore be my burden
> And more than ye know. . . .

The Old Norse is:

> Askr Yggdrasils drygir ervithi
> meirs an menn viti. . . .

Vigfusson translates: 'The ash, Ygg's steed, suffers greater hardships than men know of.' The poem is *Grimnis-Mal*, Op. cit. vol. I, p. 73.

God trembles in heaven, and his angels are white with the terror of God

> For his twilight is come on him,
> His anguish is here;
> And his spirits gaze dumb on him,
> Grown grey from his fear;
> And his hour taketh hold on him stricken, the last of his infinite year.

This refers to the God of the priests and kings and tyrants, who is so frantically denounced in the 'Hymn of Man', which at the same time announces his destruction.[1] The idea of the 'twilight of the gods', familiar to us from *Götterdämmerung*, the final opera of Wagner's Nibelungen tetralogy (which was being composed just at this time), comes from Old Norse, in which it is called 'Ragnarok'.[2]

Swinburne, of course, would have been furious to have been told that his 'death of God' was an idea which he had got from scholars of an ancient language of which he could not read one word. He would have claimed that it was inspired by the onward march, down the broadening highway of the nineteenth century, of Man, the master of things, which started in the French Revolution. And in the larger sense he would have been right. *Songs before Sunrise* is, though at a longer interval, as much the result of the French Revolution as *Prometheus Unbound*. Like *Prometheus*, it celebrates the liberation of the human spirit from all shackles, and chiefly from the shackle of the idea of God, which it had itself created. As Demogorgon says, in the marvellous litany with which *Prometheus Unbound* closes:

> Man, who wert once a despot and a slave;
> A dupe and a deceiver; a decay;
> A traveller from the cradle to the grave
> Through the dim light of this immortal day—

'Hertha,' as Gosse rightly claimed, is a profoundly philosophical poem. But before establishing that proposition, it is necessary to establish that it is NOT what it has sometimes been

---

[1] 'Man, thy slave, shall unmake thee, who made thee lord over man.' The destruction of something which, ex hypothesi, had never existed, may seem unconvincing until we remember how psychology, since Swinburne's day, has shown how man's most abject slavery may be to the creations of his own conscious, or unconscious, mind.

[2] See the *Volsunga Saga*.

claimed to be, a result of the Theory of Evolution. With the Theory of Evolution as it is connected with the name of Darwin this poem has nothing whatever to do. It could have been written exactly as it is if *The Origin of Species* had never been published. Intellectual England was shaken to its foundations by the controversies, raised by the Theory of Evolution, in the 1860s; controversies concerning the origins of man and the nature of creation. As biological phenomena, Swinburne cared for none of these things. Biology, physiology, astronomy, geology, physics, chemistry—were to him as if they had not been. Not only did he know nothing of them. Their existence and significance were matters about which, to use an ugly but expressive modern phrase, he could not have cared less. He was no more interested in the descent of man than in the square root of minus one.[1]

From which it follows that all attempts to connect 'Hertha' with the *scientific* thought of the nineteenth century are foredoomed to failure. Beach made the attempt in 1936;[2] Tillyard in 1948. To deal only with the latter (for Tillyard was a notable English scholar, albeit in a period other than the nineteenth century); it is, just, conceivably possible to ascribe to some knowledge of 'the violence of geological evolution':

> All sounds of all changes,
> All shadows and lights
> On the world's mountain ranges
> And stream-riven heights—

When we hear, of:

> First life on my sources
> First drifted and swam

that 'First life=protozoa. Swinburne knows and refers to contemporary theories of Evolution', we shall, while certainly agreeing that he knew more than enough Greek to know what protozoa meant, inevitably ask what 'contemporary theories' Tillyard had in mind, and what is his evidence that Swinburne knew them. But when we are told that:

> I am equal and whole

[1] As he was himself conscious: see Lang, No. 554.
[2] *Nature in Nineteenth Century English Poetry.*

'refers, among other things, to the conservation of energy and the indestructibility of matter', we call a halt. To convince us that Swinburne had ever heard of the second law of thermodynamics, or cared a fig for it, Tillyard would have had his work cut out. What is more to the point, the remark shows an astonishing misapprehension of the essential nature of the poem. Energy and matter, as far as 'Hertha' is concerned with them, might not exist. The poem is concerned, not with physics but with metaphysics. The Divinity-Humanity is speaking, not in terms of thermodynamics, but of ontology.

Hertha-Yggdrasil is in herself τα ὄντα, all living Reality. This is expressed in terms which, for all the difference of language are (as Tillyard rightly says) as metaphysical in essence as Donne:

> Beside or above me
>   Nought is there to go;
> Love or unlove me,
>   Unknow me or know,
> I am that which unloves me and loves; I am stricken, and I am the blow.

> I the mark that is missed
>   And the arrows that miss,
> I the mouth that is kissed
>   And the breath in the kiss,
> The search, and the sought, and the seeker, the soul and the body that is.

> I am that thing which blesses
>   My spirit elate;
> That which caresses
>   With hands uncreate
> My limbs unbegotten that measure the length of the measure of fate.

Before Humanity was, Hertha-Yggdrasil was Humanity *in posse*. When the Cosmic Process (the conception of which is implicit in the poem) in due course produced Man, she was revealed—she here reveals herself—as identical with Man *in esse*

> But what thing dost thou now,
>   Looking Godward, to cry
> 'I am I, thou art thou,
>   I am low, thou art high'?   [art I.
> I am thou, whom thou seekest to find him; find thou but thyself, thou

The author of *Atlanta in Calydon* and *Erechtheus* owed it to his love
of Hellas to make an allusion to that wonderful fruition of the
Tree of Humanity:

> In the spring-coloured hours
> When my mind was as May's,
> There brake forth of me flowers
> By centuries of days, [as rays.
> Strong blossoms with perfume of manhood, shot out from my spirit
>
> And the sound of them springing
> And smell of their shoots
> Were as warmth and sweet singing
> And strength to my roots; [my fruits.
> And the lives of my children made perfect with freedom of soul were

Reading that, we think of the promise that Swinburne, writing
some eight years after *Songs before Sunrise*, put into the mouth of
Pallas Athene: that Earth should not again behold

> So great a light alive beneath the sun
> As the aweless eye of Athens; all fame else
> Shall be to her fame as a shadow in sleep
> To this wide noon at waking. . . .

Hertha-Yggdrasil testifies that it is 'freedom of soul' which has,
in the course of the Cosmic Process, brought about the death of
God. He was but an anthropomorphism; an imperfect image of
himself which Man has now outgrown.

> Thought made him and breaks him,
> Truth slays and forgives;
> But to you, as time takes him,
> This new thing it gives,
> Even love, the belovèd Republic, that feeds upon freedom and lives.

Surely, one must say in passing, any reader with a feeling for
language must want to shout as the great fifth line comes thunder-
ing in, overwhelming and drowning all dry questions of definition
and prosaic 'meaning' in the exuberance of its seething foam. All

great poetry, in any language of which I know anything, 'means'
not only what it says, but also what it sounds.

In this remarkable poem we have, as has been said, the Creed
of the Religion of Humanity as a great poet conceived it. It is
appropriate that he should in places even have used the language
of the Liturgy:

> For Truth only is living,
> Truth only is whole. . . .

'Quoniam tu solus sanctus, tu solus Dominus. . . .'

In its intensity and its unimpeachable sincerity, this Creed recalls
the Nicene. In its elaboration, it almost recalls the Athanasian:

> 'This is the Faith of Humanity; which except a man do
> faithfully and steadfastly believe, he cannot be saved.' For

> I am in thee to save thee,
> As my soul in thee saith;
> Give thou as I gave thee,
> Thy life-blood and breath,
> Green leaves of thy labour, white flowers of thy thought, and red fruit
> of thy death.

That the colours are those of United Italy is now little to the
point. What is to the point is that a man should be willing to lay
down his life for that to which he owes his highest allegiance.

Since the third quarter of the nineteenth century there has
flourished, in many different forms, and with many various
emphases, what is essentially a Religion of Humanity. Starting as
'Positivism', it has now developed into the 'Humanist' religion
of which, in England, Sir Julian Huxley is probably the most
distinguished prophet. Before going on to consider that, however, we must consider a remarkable development which has
taken place, dating roughly from the second World War, within,
or at least upon the fringes of, the Christian Church itself. The
chief protagonists of this have been Christian ministers, or at
least theologians trained in its doctrines and proceeding from
them. I am not qualified to deal with purely theological matters;

and these pages are concerned with the history of ideas. In so far as the ideas which must now be briefly discussed are not only concerned with the same material as much of theology, but have also been formulated by professional theologians, I find myself in a dilemma. No account of the 'Religions of Humanity' in our time can pass them over entirely in silence. But I am quite incompetent to give an exposition of existentialist theology; and such an exposition would, if adequate to the subject, be out of proportion in this chapter, and indeed in this book. I am, therefore, confining myself to a purely English manifestation of it; which, involving as it did two public pronouncements by the Archbishop of Canterbury dissociating himself from it, gave the whole subject unparalleled publicity.

The development in question has now come to be called 'The Death of God'. But it is something altogether different from the rationalism and atheism which characterised the later nineteenth century. Its concomitant has been the increased emphasis placed upon the importance of Man in religion; and the concern of the theologians with human psychology and human relationships. What we have here is essentially one of the mid-twentieth century versions of the Religion of Humanity. It springs fundamentally from three sources: in the first place, it is a total reaction from the famous 'Theology of Crisis' of Karl Barth; which was itself partly a reaction from 'pantheistic' Bergsonian ideas; but above all a product of the first World War. The essence of Barth's theology has been described as: 'the overwhelming love of the absolutely supreme, transendent God, who comes in infinite condescension to give himself to man in unconditional freedom and grace'.[1] In the second place, the 'Death of God' theologians are permeated by the existentialism which has played so large a part in Western thought since the second World War. Finally, they have been much influenced by what is most conveniently called 'depth psychology'.

Outside theological circles, the whole movement had, in England, attracted little attention until 1963. In March of that year there was published a book entitled *Honest to God*, by John Robinson, then Suffragan Bishop of Woolwich. Though containing little that was new, and hardly anything of intellectual value, this book produced in the Anglican church a furore

[1] Obituary notice of Karl Barth in the *Times*, December 11, 1968.

unparalleled since *Essays and Reviews*. Nor was its effect confined to professing Christians. It revealed the interest of an enormous, officially non-religious, public in religion. In the last five years, it has sold over a million copies and been translated into many languages. In it, the author attempts, not to 'destroy' God, after the manner of the rationalist atheists; but to replace what he considers to be an erroneous conception of God, by another, based upon an existentialist interpretation of Man's own nature. Although by far its most sensational manifestation, this book is really wholly derivative from the 'Death of God' school; which, comparatively unknown to the general reading public of England until Dr. Robinson made it famous, has been one of the most notable developments in theology since the Second World War.

In a second book, *The Honest to God Debate* (1965), there were printed many of the reactions to the first; ranging from authoritative reviews by theologians of recognised standing to private letters sent to Dr. Robinson. They show that he has had both great success with some readers, and complete failure with others. Dr. Robinson is dismissed as merely one of the 'angry young men' of the fifties and sixties by C. Booker in *The Neophyliacs* (Collins, 1969, p. 190).

Before attempting to outline what appears to be the main thesis of *Honest to God*, historical accuracy as well as fairness to Dr. Robinson require it to be made clear that he makes no claim to be the original author of the ideas he expounds. What he was attempting was primarily a popularisation, involving a certain amount of synthesis. Above all, as a leading churchman, he considered it his duty to offer help to those to whom the traditional conception of God seemed, as he thought, to be proving a stumbling block. Of that he writes as follows:

> 'I am firmly convinced that this whole way of thinking can be the greatest obstacle to an intelligent faith—indeed will progressively be so to all except the 'religious' few. We shall eventually be no more able to convince men of the existence of a God 'out there' whom they must call in to order their lives than persuade them to take seriously the gods of Olympus. If Christianity is to survive, let alone to recapture 'secular' man, there is no time to lose in detaching it from this scheme of thought.[1]

[1] *Honest to God*, p. 43.

He gives a very interesting account of the sources of his ideas; of these, only three authors will here be mentioned, though there were several other, less important, ones.

The first of these in date for me (though not in composition) was a sermon by Paul Tillich, which appeared in his collection *The Shaking of the Foundations*, published in England in 1949 (now available in a Pelican edition). It was called 'The Depth of Existence', and it opened my eyes to the transformation that seemed to come over so much of the traditional religious symbolism when it was transposed from the heights to the depths. God, Tillich was saying, is not a projection 'out there', an Other beyond the skies, of whose existence we have to convince ourselves, but the Ground of our very being.[1] He then proceeds to quote Tillich (the italics for the pronouns are mine):

The name of this infinite and inexhaustible depth and ground of all being is *God*. That depth is what the word *God* means. And if that word has not such meaning for *you*, translate it, and speak of the depths of *your* life, of the source of *your* being, of *your* ultimate concern, of what *you* take seriously without any reservation. Perhaps, in order to do so, you must forget everything traditional that you have learned about God, perhaps even that word itself.

There are many other quotations from Tillich in *Honest to God*, but this will suffice for our purpose.

The second source to which Robinson acknowledges his indebtedness is Dietrich Bonhoeffer, a German Protestant pastor, born in 1906 and hanged in a Nazi concentration camp in 1945 (for alleged participation in the plot against Hitler). His now famous *Letters and Papers from Prison* first appeared in an English version in 1953 (ed. E. Bethge; the American edition is entitled *Prisoner for God*). Robinson says that he first encountered extracts from this book in the *Ecumenical Review* in 1952, and adds:

One felt at once that the Church was not yet ready for what Bonhoeffer was giving us as his last will and testament before he was hanged by the S.S.: indeed, it might be understood properly only a hundred years hence.[2]

[1] Ibid, p. 21–2.
[2] Op. cit., p. 23.

From the numerous references to, and quotations from, Bonhoeffer, and of course because of them (since for one reader of Bonhoeffer there must be a thousand of Robinson), it has come to be very widely assumed that the two fundamental propositions upon which Bonhoeffer's position rests are these:

(i) Man has 'come of age', and outgrown the need for God.
(ii) The only true Christianity is 'religionless'.

While it may indeed require a hundred years to understand the second of these, since, as our brains are now constituted, it is, as it stands, nonsense, the first proposition is nothing new. It is to be found, prosaically and dogmatically, stated by Comte; and imaginatively and poetically by Swinburne. These two propositions are fundamental to Robinson's main thesis in *Honest to God*.[1]

To a third source, Robinson acknowledges his debt as follows:

> There was an essay which created an almost immediate explosion when it appeared in 1941, though I did not read it in detail till it was translated into English in 1953. This was the manifesto by Rudolf Bultmann entitled 'New Testament and Mythology' (in *Kerygma and Myth*, ed. Bartsch, vol. I, pp. 1–44) (In this, the 'mythological' element in the New Testament is examined). . . . And his contention was that this whole element is unintelligible jargon to the modern man.[2]

---

[1] It has been several times pointed out that they are largely a misunderstanding of Bonhoeffer (who in any case had no time for a full formulation of his thought). The clearest writer to do so is the Reader in Religious Studies in the University of Sussex. In the *Times* of 2nd March, 1968 Daniel Jenkins wrote:

'His main preoccupation in these letters is the same as it was throughout his life, that of discovering what it means to be a follower of Christ. He says that, partly through his experience of living outside ecclesiastical circles, he had become very critical of 'religion' and speaks of holding the Christian faith without the 'religious pre-supposition'. This is a statement which causes legitimate bewilderment unless it is realised that he is speaking of 'religion' in a limited sense which would be more familiar to the German theological friend to whom he was writing than it is to the British reader.

It is religion understood as the attempt of man to reach God on the basis of an acknowledgement of his own weakness and inadequacy, which makes him aware of the need for a Power greater than himself upon whom we can depend. . . . He claims that it is wrong to suppose that Christian faith is dependent for its efficacy upon making people conscious of their weakness. Its concern is with the recovery of freedom and proper humanity. It should recognise that man has now come of age and should speak to him in his strength. What exactly he meant by this 'coming of age' he was not permitted to make clear, but it evidently involves the acceptance of man's autonomy.'

[2] P. 24.

Some pages later, there is an even more revealing passage: Bultmann answers boldly 'there is nothing specifically Christian in the mythical view of the world as such. It is simply the cosmology of a pre-scientific age'. 'The New Testament,' he says, 'presents redemption in Christ as a supernatural event—as the incarnation from "the other side" of a celestial Being who enters this earthly scene through a miraculous birth, performs signs and wonders as an indication of his heavenly origin, and after an equally miraculous resurrection returns by ascent to the celestial sphere whence he came'. In truth, Bultmann maintains, all this language is not, properly speaking, describing a supernatural transaction of any kind, but is an attempt to express the real depth, dimension and significance of the *historical* event of Jesus Christ. In this person and event there was something of ultimate, unconditional significance for human life—and that, translated into the mythological view of the world, comes out as 'God' (a Being up there) 'sending' (to 'this' world) his only begotten 'Son'. The transcendental significance of the historical event is 'objectivised' as a supernatural transaction?

We must now address ourselves to Robinson himself, and attempt an exposition of his views; but fortunately only in so far as they are concerned with God. The second half of the book is beyond our purview. *Honest to God* is the least lucid religious or philosophical work that I have ever read. When it comes to what Robinson calls 'Christology' (by which he, who is after all a Bishop of a Christian church, means reconciliation of his views with the orthodox doctrine of that church), the mental contortions into which he is forced become painful to contemplate. This obscurity is, every now and then, riven by a lurid flash of wit—when the lightning of his intellect is summoned to destroy the obscurantists. Here, for example, is how he describes the orthodox view of the Incarnation ('which most people, and I include myself, have been brought up to believe at Christmas time'): 'God took a space trip and arrived on this planet where he appeared dressed up like Father Xmas.'

Another, if less brilliant, flash is the description of:

> The Deist conception of God's relation to the world. Here God is the supreme Being, the grand Architect, who exists somewhere out beyond the world—like a rich Aunt in Australia

G

—who started it all going, periodically intervenes in its running, and generally gives evidence of his benevolent interest in it.[1]

In *Honest to God*, not only is there no rich aunt in Australia, nor uncle either. There is not one anywhere. We are told over and over again *ad nauseam* that spatial imagery is inadmissible. You must not think of God as 'up there', 'out there', or 'over there' (the prophet's reference to 'The High and Holy One that inhabiteth eternity', which some of us thought we understood, is presumably 'unintelligible jargon'). You must not think of 'Him' at all, because there is no such Person—or even 'It' (unless you can achieve the considerable feat of conceiving an 'It' which is at once nowhere and everywhere). Robinson gives, and will admit, only two formulations of what God is (which he gives in at least half a dozen places). Here they are:

(i) God is Ultimate Reality—and Ultimate Reality is God.
(ii) God is the Ground of Your Being—and the Ground of Your Being is God.

Of these two propositions, the first is simply a truncated version of the classical ontological 'proof' of God's existence, but so stated that it is merely a flat assertion, with no logical cogency whatever. The second is nothing else than what the divinity Hertha-Yggdrasill, in incomparably more eloquent language, said to Man:

I am thou, whom thou seekest to find him; find thou but thyself, thou art I.

We come back essentially to the Religion of Humanity. In its early days, it was expressed in terms of 'Positivism'. That is now out of fashion. Its place has been taken by psychology and existentialism. In the early summer of 1967, there was published in England a book entitled *The God I Want*, which perfectly illustrates the point. It is a symposium of nine essays, two of them by women (one of which, by Miss Bernadine Bishop, appeared in the *Times*). The real interest of this book, at least to me, lies less in the substance of what these writers say than in the manner in which they approach their subject. The great theologians of the Middle Ages, who produced the five famous 'proofs' of the existence of God, considered the matter in philosophical and metaphysical terms. With one notable exception, Mr. H. A.

[1] P. 30.

Williams, then Dean of Trinity College, Cambridge (whose essay is altogether in a class of its own), none of the contributors to *The God I Want* would, I think, claim to have much philosophical equipment. Nor did they consider it necessary. For to them, the ontological, the teleological, the cosmological and the rest, are of no interest. Their supreme concern is with the psychological. I am not qualified to judge of their equipment in psychology; though I suspect that only one of them, a professional psychologist, could make any substantial claim in this respect; and his essay is mainly an amplification of the statement that the God he does NOT want is the sort of God most of his patients try to turn him into. But you do not nowadays need to have had psychological training to use the technical vocabulary of psychology. The contributors to *The God I Want* bring to the discussion of the existence and nature of God such phrases as: 'The resolution of the Oedipus complex', 'the sublimation of the Id', 'the assertion of the Super-ego', and so on. To say this is not to deride them. They are all highly intelligent and deeply sincere. It is merely to illustrate the contemporary cast of thought.

Whither this road, once taken, inexorably leads is shown by Sir Julian Huxley, in an essay entitled 'The New Divinity', of which more must be said later.[1] The Book of Genesis describes the final stage in the process of creation thus:

> And God said, Let us make man in our image, after our likeness.

Sir Julian writes:

> God is a hypothesis constructed by man to help him understand what existence is all about.

The wheel has come full circle. It might be put thus: 'And man said, Let us make God in our image, after our likeness.'

None of the authors of *The God I Want* goes as far as this. They might be happier and more convincing if they did. For, with the exception of two avowed Christians and one avowed atheist, the fundamental complaint of all of them is thus described by Miss Bishop:

[1] See p. 89.

Something has gone wrong with God. We cannot be his saviours, shoring what fragments we can merely because we have been landed with institutional churches. God has become for most people, and even for many practising Christians, unreal. The God we want must be real. He must be a convincing personal experience.

There we have it. God must be 'a convincing personal experience'. In order to get it, modern, urbanised, so-called civilised western man summons to his aid not only psychology but also existentialism. 'If I am to believe in God,' he says, 'then the evidence must come from what I know of my own existence. Nay, more: if God, as far as I am concerned (and if I am not concerned then the whole business has for me no meaning), if God *has* any existence, then he must, in some way that is real, even though it may elude expression in human language, be at least in part my own existence'.

We are here getting into waters which the psychologist is as incapable of plumbing as the metaphysician. But what is to our present purpose is that here, by a different route, we have met an old friend: no less than Dr. John Robinson, Bishop of Woolwich. The nub of what he said in *Honest to God* was this: It is no use looking for God in the physical Universe. You will not find him. God is the ground of *your* being; and the ground of *your* being is God. At this point, a quotation may be given from the article by Mr. H. A. Williams in *The God I Want:*

Dr. Robinson is right in insisting that the God apparently apprehended as independent of myself out there, is an illusion. But what Dr. Robinson has not seen, or at least not clearly emphasised, is that to discover God as myself is also to discover him as other than myself.

In *Honest to God* Dr. Robinson asks—I paraphrase several passages —'How if you cannot find God in the Universe? He is neither up there, nor out there, nor down there. How if the heavens are empty? What then?' This question, as *The God I Want* abundantly shows, is a matter of the deepest moment to thinking men and women. My own answer to Dr. Robinson would be somewhat as follows:

You tell me that God is not to be found in the Universe, but that he is Ultimate Reality. No human intellect is capable of comprehending either of these statements. Both of us, however, are perfectly capable of understanding the inevitable logical deduction from these premises: which is that God is transcendent to the Universe. This view was generally held until the 17th century. But you also tell me that God is the ground of my being. You cannot know this, since neither you nor any man knows what consciousness is; but Descartes went a long way to showing that my own self-consciousness is the best proof of my existence. Since the time of Descartes, evidence has been accumulating, and is now overwhelming, that consciousness is the end-product of that Process which is all that the unaided mind of Man is ever likely to comprehend of the nature of the Universe—in which, you confidently tell me, I shall not find God. The intellectual value of your formulations concerning God does not seem to me worth the price. For, whether you admit it or not, there is a price to be paid: no less than the integrity of Christian profession. How can you reconcile your muddled metaphysics with what the Founder of our religion told us about his Father: 'Blessed are the pure in heart *for they shall see God*'?

Towards the end of 1967, Dr. Robinson produced yet another book, *Exploration into God*. Although the lucidity and cogency which he had when he was a New Testament scholar seem to have permanently departed from him, this is a better book than *Honest to God*. Its author describes it as 'more fundamental and more radical'. It is at least more convincing. Recapitulating and amplifying his own objections to theism, Dr. Robinson now professes allegiance to panentheism; which he describes as 'the view that God is in everything and everything is in God', differentiating it from pantheism in holding that: 'his Being is more than, and is not exhausted by, the Universe' (p. 83–4). The considerable dilemmas into which such a belief lands him— notably that of the problem of suffering and 'prevenient intention' —need not here concern us. What is pertinent is his apparent conversion to some form of belief in Cosmic Process. *Honest to God* contained nothing of the kind. But, now that he has ceased to churn out slogans about God, and has begun to enquire into realities, Dr. Robinson reaches deeper levels. He also makes it quite clear that, whatever may have been the case some years ago, he is now most definitely NOT a disciple of the Religion of Humanity. He seems to be becoming one of Cosmic Process.

He will have nothing to do with a 'God-who-becomes'. This is stated categorically: 'The creative Ground is not identified with the process, like the emergent Deity in some forms of Bergsonian pantheism; the Creator is not created, God is not evolved' (p. 99–100). But the conception of a Cosmic Process through which 'the creative Ground' operates is clearly enunciated. And it is most interesting that this is done in connection with a passage which he explicitly repudiated in *Honest to God*, the beginning of the Fourth Gospel. In the earlier book he wrote: 'If Christianity is to survive, let alone recapture "secular" man, there is no time to lose in detaching it from this scheme of thought, from this particular theology of *logos* about *theos*, and thinking hard about what he should put in its place' (*Honest to God*, p. 43). In his *Systematic Theology*, vol. 3, p. 307, Tillich (whom Dr. Robinson quotes when it suits him) says: He who sacrifices the Logos principle sacrifices the idea of a living God, and he who rejects the application of this principle to Jesus as the Christ rejects his character as Christ.

From what he writes in *Exploration into God*, it is evident that this thinking has been taking place, and has not been unfruitful. In the latter book he writes (italics mine):

'My concern . . . is to relate the Christian interpretation of creation to the panentheistic rather than to the theistic projection. First, I should like to attempt to rephrase the Biblical passage which above all is trying to express the conviction that *the entire process of nature and history* is to be viewed, not only, to use Teilhard de Chardin's categories, in terms of 'hominization' but of 'Christification'. This will frankly be a paraphrase, not a translation, and is not meant to be taken as exegesis. But it may help to interpret what was *intended* to be *a cosmic panorama in terms of modern evolutionary cosmogony*. The passage is, of course, the prologue to St. John's Gospel'.

Here is the beginning of Dr. Robinson's paraphrase:

'The clue to the Universe as personal was present from the beginning. It was to be found at the level of reality which we call God. Indeed, it was no other than God nor God than it. At that depth of reality the element of the personal was there from the start. Everything was drawn into existence through it, and *there is nothing in the process that has come into being without it*. Life owes its emergence to it, and life lights the path to man. It is that light which illumines the darkness of the sub-personal creation, and the darkness never succeeded in quenching it.'

It can be freely and gratefully acknowledged that the author of that paraphrase is much nearer to the fundamental truth of the religion that he professes than he ever came in *Honest to God*.

The quotation, some pages back, from Sir Julian Huxley, about God being a hypothesis invented by man to explain existence, is taken from the Essay entitled "The New Divinity" in *Essays of a Humanist*.

In the course of it, he refers to the implications of 'Dr. Robinson's courageous book', and then makes the following very cogent criticism; the implications of which will lead us naturally to consider briefly Huxley's own 'Humanist Religion', with which we shall conclude this chapter:

Dr. Robinson is surely right in concentrating on the problem of God, rather than the resurrection or the after-life, for God is Christianity's central hypothesis. But he is surely wrong in making such statements as that 'God is ultimate reality'. God is a hypothesis constructed by man to help him understand what existence is all about. The god hypothesis asserts the existence of some sort of supernatural or superpersonal being, exerting some kind of purposeful power over the universe and its destiny. To say that God is ultimate reality is just semantic cheating, as well as being so vague as to become effectively meaningless (and when Dr. Robinson continues by saying 'and ultimate reality must exist' he is surely running round a philosophically very vicious circle).

Dr. Robinson, like Dr. Tillich and many other modernist theologians, seems to me, and indeed to any humanist, to be trying to ride two horses at once, to keep his cake and eat it. He wants to be modern and meet the challenge of our new knowledge by stripping the image of God of virtually all its spatial, material, mythological, Freudian and anthropomorphic aspects. But he still persists in retaining the term *God*, in spite of all its implications of supernatural power and personality; and it is these implications, not the modernists' fine-spun arguments, which consciously or unconsciously affect the ordinary man and woman. Heads I win, tails you lose; humanists dislike this elaborate double-talk (p. 221).

Our first two chapters attempted to outline, by selective examples, the rise of the conception of Cosmic Process. In Goethe, this conception emerges very clearly, though in his lifetime it was only beginning to be formulated in terms of the Theory of Evolution. That theory completely dominated two thirds of the nineteenth century; and the poetry of Tennyson most strikingly illustrates how, not only in its biological but also in its astronomical and geological aspects, it profoundly affected his whole conception of the nature and meaning of the Universe. The present chapter has tried to trace briefly the emergence of the conception of Man, the end-product of the evolutionary process, as the most advanced form of life of which we have knowledge; whom, therefore Comte, considering Humanity as a collective whole, termed 'The Great Being', who must replace a fictitious 'God' as the object of our veneration and worship. Swinburne carried much further the idea that the very conception of God was the creation of Man's imagination; and must be discarded now that Man has reached maturity. And Swinburne expressed this, which was to him an emotion rather than a metaphysic, in form and language much more suited to preaching a religion than was the language employed by Comte. In *Honest to God* we find a Christian priest (in company with many others) attempting to deal with this situation in our own day; and trying to reconcile it with the basic doctrines of his own religion. The attempt to retain God, by a process of depersonalisation, because without God the foundations of the Christian religion collapse, appears to Julian Huxley 'just semantic cheating'. He himself proclaims a 'Humanist Religion' which dispenses entirely with what Laplace, in reply to an enquiry as to God's place in the 'Celestial Mechanics' is reputed to have called 'That hypothesis'. Nearly two centuries ago, Voltaire wrote 'Si Dieu n'existait pas, il faudrait l'inventer'. The contemporary Humanists would say that if God had not been invented, it would not now be necessary to abolish him.

It need hardly be said that Julian Huxley has an intellect of the first order. That he is one of the most eminent Englishmen of our time he owes chiefly to his work as a biologist. In addition to his gifts as a scientist, he has all the creative imagination of his brother Aldous (though he uses it to entirely different ends); and all the trenchancy of the famous grandfather of them both, Thomas Henry, without the belligerency produced in *him* by having to do constant battle with the obscurantism of a whole generation. Julian Huxley has been preaching the Humanist religion for more than 30 years. Over that period, he has published a number of notable books on the subject.[1] To them must be referred anyone wishing to obtain a grasp of it. All that can be attempted here is to illustrate some of his fundamental tenets by a few quotations from his latest *Essays of a Humanist*. Mere extracts from such closely-knit arguments are inevitably unsatisfactory. But with a writer of such clarity and cogency, it seems better to let him speak in his own words than attempt an inferior summary.

One thing must be added. He has always been intensely interested in Man; not only as the most fascinating of all biological specimens, but also as infinitely the most advanced of all social animals—and in all the implications of those facts. His whole life-long standpoint can be summed up in the title of a collection of Essays published in 1941: *The Uniqueness of Man*.[2] In the Preface to that volume he wrote:

> The most vital task of the present age is to formulate a social base for civilisation, to dethrone economic ideals and replace them by human ones.

This endeavour to find *human* ideals as the bases for civilisation has been the driving force behind his crusade for the Humanistic religion. How deep and wide a sense the word 'human' has for Julian Huxley will, it is hoped, emerge even from the following (necessarily meagre) extracts.

The first, from the Essay 'The Humanist Frame,' is concerned with what are the present requirements of Man:

> He needs to use his best efforts of knowledge and imagination to build a system of thought and belief which will provide both a supporting framework for his present existence, an ultimate or ideal goal for his future development as a species, and a guide and directive for practical action and planning. This new idea-system, whose birth we of the mid-twentieth

---

[1] To mention only the most important: *Religion without Revelation* (1928); *Man in the Modern World* (1947); *Evolution in Action* (1951): *New Bottles for New Wine* (1957).

[2] The essay bearing this title is chiefly devoted to the momentous results of man's having acquired the power of speech. This enables him to formulate, record and transmit conceptual thought.

century are witnessing, I shall simply call *Humanism*, because it can only be based on our understanding of man and his relations with the rest of his environment. It must be focussed on man as an organism, though one with unique properties. It must be organised round the facts and ideas of evolution, taking account of the discovery that man is part of a comprehensive evolutionary process, and cannot avoid playing a decisive role in it.[1]

The second is an explanation of why Humanists cannot subscribe to the traditional doctrines of Christian theology:

A theological system incorporating such beliefs has a number of consequences which Humanists find undesirable. The belief in supernatural beings capable of affecting human destiny leads to petitionary rather than aspirational prayer, and to all kinds of propitiatory practices. . . . Belief in a supernatural after-life leads to concentration on attaining salvation in the other world and to a lack of concern for life in this world and its possible improvement. Belief in the fall of man and the necessity of redemption through an incarnate divine Saviour has led to the cruel (and untrue) doctrines of Original Sin and Damnation for unbelievers. . . .

Above all, belief in an omnipotent, omniscient and omnibenevolent God leads to a frustrating dilemma at the very heart of our approach to reality. For many thinking people, it is incompatible with our knowledge of nature and history and with the facts of evil, suffering and human misery. Even when, as in some modernist versions of Christian theology, the idea of a personal God is watered down and transmogrified into some abstract principle of supposed Absolute behind phenomena, and the Deity is removed further and further from any possibility of active interference in natural or human events, the dilemma remains. The human mind and spirit is not interested in such a Pickwickian God, and refuses to be fobbed off by assertions as to our inherent incapacity to understand Him (p. 105).

The third extract deals with realities which, having been wrongly formulated by the Christian theologians, need now to be re-formulated, correctly, by the Humanists:

[1] *Essays of a Humanist*, p. 73. When, as here, part of one paragraph only is quoted, and continued into part of the next, I do not observe the original paragraphing.

Religious concepts like god, incarnation, the soul, salvation, original sin, grace, atonement, all have a basis in man's experiences of phenomenal reality. It is necessary now to analyse that basis of reality into its component parts, and then to reassemble these elements, together with any new factors that have come to light, into concepts which correspond more closely to reality and are more relevant to present circumstances. . . . The forces are real enough: what we have done, quite illegitimately, is to project the god concept into them. And in so doing we have distorted their true significance, and effectively altered the course of history.

Once this is realised, it should be possible to reformulate such ideas as Divine Law, obedience to God's will, or union with the mind of God, in an evolutionary terminology consonant with existing scientific knowledge.

Again, Christian ethics (to which the world owes a great debt) are based on the doctrine of Original Sin resulting from the Fall of Man. This is an attempt to provide an acceptable interpretation of such general and well nigh universal phenomena as our sense of guilt, our search for atonement and for some form of salvation, our authoritarian consciences, our rigorous sense of right and wrong, our consequent persecution of those who deviate from what we feel is the right path (p. 109).

It will be seen that, to the formidable mental equipment which his grandfather possessed, Julian Huxley has added knowledge which was not available in the days of his grandfather: knowledge, though still incomplete, of the nature and modes of operation of human personality, which has been revealed by the investigations of psychology. Near the conclusion of this essay, he sets forth the purpose of his new Religion of Humanity:

The central belief of Evolutionary Humanism is that existence can be improved, that vast untapped possibilities can be increasingly realised, that greater fulfilment can replace frustration. This belief is now firmly grounded in knowledge: it could become in turn the firm ground for action (p. 115).

Another Essay in this volume, 'The New Divinity', which has already been quoted, opens (after the initial reference to the Bishop of Woolwich and the theological ferment of our time) with a passage so striking that it must be quoted. Above all, it illustrates to perfection the position now attained by the conception of Cosmic Process, the growth of which it has been the purpose of these pages to trace:

> This is the inevitable outcome of the new vision of the world and man's place and role in that world—in a word, of man's destiny—which our new knowledge has revealed. This new vision is both comprehensive and unitary. It integrates the fantastic diversity of the world into a single framework, the pattern of *all-embracing evolutionary process*. In this unitary vision, all kinds of splits and dualisms are healed. The entire cosmos is made out of one and the same world-stuff, operated by the same energy as we ourselves. 'Mind' and 'matter' appear as two aspects of our unitary mind-bodies. There is no separate supernatural realm: all phenomena are part of *one natural process of evolution*. There is no basic cleavage between science and religion; they are both organs of evolving humanity.
>
> This earth is one of the rare spots in the cosmos where mind has flowered. Man is a product of nearly three billion years of evolution, *in whose person the evolutionary process has at last become conscious of itself and its possibilities*. Whether he likes it or not, he is responsible for the whole further evolution of our planet (p. 218. Italics mine).

CHAPTER FOUR

'ALPHA AND OMEGA'
THE VISION OF PIERRE TEILHARD DE CHARDIN

In 1955 there was published in Paris, posthumously, a book entitled *Le Phénomène humain*, by Pierre Teilhard de Chardin. More than a decade later, it can be confidently affirmed that this book not only is, but has now been generally acknowledged as, one of the outstanding works of our time. This recognition is in no way diminished by a few strident voices proclaiming that it is nothing but trash; and sometimes adding, for good measure, what fools most of the intellectuals of Europe and America must be, to be taken in by it. What we have here is the modern version of 'odium theologicum', which has now become 'antitheologicum'. The fact that no intelligent person could possibly accept the main thesis of *Le Phénomène humain*, and continue to regard the Universe as wholly mechanistic is, to these detractors, as a red rag to a bull. Their real trouble is that, to counter Teilhard's thesis, they have no credible antithesis. The Universe of the later nineteenth century materialist, a wholly mechanistic structure composed of atoms, which are the ultimate constituents of the Universe, has collapsed about the ears of any who believed in it. It would, perhaps, be more appropriate to say that it has vanished in a flash, and left nothing behind. For what it has left behind is 'Energy'. What that essentially is, no man knows. What we do know (and it would have made Haeckel gasp) is that the clearest formulation of the nature of Matter that any contemporary scientist would attempt would have to be made largely in terms of Energy. And Energy, as we shall see, was one of Teilhard's main preoccupations.

Teilhard was a scientist; by the end of his life an anthropologist with a world-wide reputation. He was also a Jesuit priest. Born in 1881, one of eleven children of a small landowner in Auvergne, he was educated at a Jesuit college, joined the Society of Jesus at eighteen and took a triple vow of chastity, poverty and obedience after his ordination in 1912. He had periods of study in Jersey and Sussex, and taught physics and chemistry in a Jesuit

Collège in Cairo. He studied in Paris under Marcellin Boule, and during the first World War was a stretcher bearer, gaining the Médail militaire and the Legion d'Honneur. He became Professor of Geology at the Catholic Institute in Paris, and took his Doctorate at the Sorbonne in 1922. In 1923 he went for a year to China. On his return to Paris he was forbidden to continue teaching on account of some of the ideas expressed in his lectures concerning Original Sin and its relation to Evolution (in which he had, before ordination, become profoundly interested as a result of reading Bergson).[1] In 1926 he returned to work in China; where, with brief intervals, he was destined to remain for twenty years. The outbreak of the second World War prevented his taking up an appointment as Director of the Laboratory of advanced studies in Geology and Palaeontology in Paris. By 1938, he had written the most important of his books, *Le Phénomène humain*.[2]

He never received permission from the Roman Catholic authorities to publish any of his major works, and on his return to Paris after the war was forbidden by them to write any more on philosophical subjects. He was also forbidden to put forward his candidature for a Professorship in the Collège de France, in succession to the Abbé Breuil—his lifelong friend. He was, however, elected Membre de l'Institut. In 1951 he moved to New York; and for the last years of his life found shelter with the Wenner-Gren Foundation, who had sponsored two previous visits to study Palaeontology in South Africa. He left all his manuscripts to a friend. After his death, two highly distinguished international Committees, one scientific and one general, were set up to sponsor the publication of his writings. The first so to be published was *Le Phénomène humain*.[3] The official English translation, under the title 'The Phenomenon of Man', first appeared

---

[1] There is an exhaustive and detailed study of the relation of Teilhard's thought to that of Bergson in M. Barthélemy-Madaule: *Bergson et Teilhard de Chardin* (Paris, Ed. du Seuil, 1963). See also Emile Rideau: *La Pensée du Père Teilhard de Chardin* (same publisher, 1965). An English translation appeared in 1967 (Collins).

[2] All the major works of Teilhard are in process of publication by Editions du Seuil. There are so far ten volumes. Of these, at least half consist of material not fully prepared by Teilhard for publication. The most important, after *Le Phénomène humain*, is probably *Le Milieu divin* (1960). Of the English translation of this, the *Times* critic wrote that it 'will certainly take its place among the rare spiritual classics of the twentieth century'. The only one of Teilhard's works considered here is *Le Phénomène humain*.

[3] All the page references given by me are to the French text of 1955, where will be found the original of the passage given by me in English.

at the end of 1959, with a most interesting Introduction by Sir Julian Huxley, who had personally known Teilhard in his later years, and been greatly impressed, and considerably influenced, by him. This translation is good; but I do not find it verbally near enough to the original; and in the pages that follow shall use my own version, unless otherwise stated.

No book yet published is so perfect an example of Man's conception of Cosmic Process in the mid-twentieth century. As Sir Julian says, Teilhard sees everything 'sub specie evolutionis'. And here is a paragraph from Teilhard himself:

'Evolution—is it a theory, a system, a hypothesis? By no means. But, much more than that, it is a general condition with which henceforth all theories, all systems, all hypotheses must comply, which they must satisfy if they are to be credible, let alone true. A light which illuminates every fact, a curve which every feature must assume; that is what Evolution is' (p. 242).

The two most striking, and original, propositions put forward by Teilhard—later to be recounted in greater detail—can be summarised thus:

(i) The fact of Consciousness in Man, and even in the animals of a sufficiently high order for it to be certainly claimed for them, cannot be explained by Science in its present terms. This fact has implications which Science has so far refused to recognize.

(ii) The evolution of Man, hitherto chiefly of a purely genetic nature, must now be regarded as becoming progressively exosomatic, or, to use Sir Julian Huxley's word 'psychosocial'. It is still, as far as we can see it in perspective, in a very early stage; and will inevitably lead to results which we can now but dimly conceive.[1]

It should here be added that not the least of the changes which our human perspective has undergone in the twentieth century is that of terrestrial time (to say nothing of extra terrestrial space-time). In the seventeenth century, it was held that the world had

[1] Genetic evolution is the result of bio-chemical processes (e.g. the influence of chromosomes). Its most obvious results are physical modifications, such as that which produced the upright position and enlarged brains of the immediate ancestors of Homo Sapiens. Exosomatic, or psychosocial, evolution is the result of the conscious exercise of Man's intelligence (e.g. eugenics). Evolution of this kind was clearly at work early in human history (e.g. the development of hunters into pastoral, and later urban, communities).

been created in 4004 B.C.,[1] and that the generation then living would have not more than four or five successors before the End of the World. The astronomers now tell us that, short of an accident, Man has a future of at least some hundreds of millions of years. It is in that perspective that Teilhard makes his propositions.

For the exposition of his ideas, Teilhard had to use a terminology containing very unusual words. A number of words he had actually to invent. The most important of these are the following (more or less in the order in which they appear in the book):

Lithosphere. He uses this to describe the condition of the Earth when it first solidified. Its chemical constitution must then have been simple, consisting of the small molecules of inorganic compounds (when they began to combine) of such elements as silicon. This state of the Earth he describes as 'State Alpha'—in contrast to the other end of terrestrial time, which he calls 'Point Omega'. With the earliest part of *Le Phénomène humain*, dealing with this 'Lithospheric' condition, I shall concern myself no further.

Biosphere. This is the name given to what he describes as the layer of organic Life that eventually spread over the Earth. Its prerequisite was the formation of extremely complex macromolecules of such organic compounds as protein.

Noosphere. This is the unitary layer of conscious Thought which, according to Teilhard, is now the supremely important and significant phenomenon on Earth. It is in the Noosphere that there became possible that ascent of Man which he calls *Hominization*.

A number of other words, such as *Complexification, Psychogenesis, mega-Synthesis*, explain themselves in their contexts. The book is divided into four main sections:

1. Before Life
2. Life

---

[1] It was James Ussher (or Usher), (1581–1656), Archbishop of Armagh, who first propounded this date, and a whole scheme of Biblical chronology in *Annales Veteris et Novi Testamenti* (1650–54). This, or something on a similar time-scale, is that of the philosophical writers of the seventeenth century in England (e.g. Sir Thomas Browne, who wrote *Religio Medici*, posthumously published). We now know that the history of Homo Sapiens alone is many times five thousand years; and Homo Sapiens was the final product of an organic evolution of hundreds of millions of years; which itself only began after the immense period needed for the Earth to reach the physical conditions necessary to its beginning.

3. Thought

4. The Future of Life.

The first of these consists of three chapters. Of these, the first is concerned with the inorganic Matter which makes up the Universe, and the third with the youth of the Earth ('la Terre juvénile'). It is the substance of the second chapter which is crucial for the later development of Teilhard's thought. Moreover, it is here that his originality, and the unconventional nature of his main thesis, really appear. The essence of this second chapter must therefore be given. The French title is 'Le Dedans des Choses'. There is no wholly satisfactory English translation for the two nouns 'Le Dedans' and 'Le Dehors'. The official translation uses 'The Within' and 'The Without'. In Teilhard's context, I prefer 'The Inwardness' and 'The Outwardness'; and shall use these words in the pages that follow.

In his chapter 'The Inwardness of Things', Teilhard points out that, for over a century, there has been a continuing controversy between the materialists, and those who hold a spiritual view of the nature of Reality; in which neither side has really met the other on its own ground. Until they do, there can be no convincing explanation of the Cosmic Phenomenon in its entirety.

'My conviction is that these two points of view need to come together, and that they will soon come together in a kind of Phenomenology, or generalised Physics, which will take into consideration the internal face of things as well as the external face of the world. Otherwise, it seems to me, it will be impossible to include in one coherent explanation, of the sort which Science owes to itself to produce, the Cosmic Phenomenon taken as a whole'. (p. 49).

The lines along which Teilhard envisages such a synthesis are broadly as follows:

Consciousness in the higher forms of life, above all self-consciousness in Man, has hitherto been eliminated by Science from its formulation of the structure of the Universe, on the ground that it was 'a bizarre exception, an aberrant function, an epiphenomenon' (p. 51). What, asks Teilhard, would have happened to modern physics had Radium been classified, on its discovery, as something abnormal and to be ignored, because it

H

fitted into no known category of elements? Being measurable mathematically, radio-activity had to be accepted as one of the properties of Matter. 'Consciousness, however, would, for its integration into the world structure, oblige us to envisage the existence of an entirely new aspect, or dimension, of the stuff of the Universe. We recoil from the effort'. Teilhard, however, does not recoil. From the undeniable self-consciousness of Mind, he extrapolates to the entire Universe. The stuff of the Universe, he says, always and everywhere, has two aspects. 'Co-existent with their Outwardness, there is an Inwardness of things' (p. 53).

At this point, Teilhard quotes in a note some words written by J. B. S. Haldane in an 'Essay on Science and Ethics' published in *The Inequality of Man* (Chatto, 1932, p. 113):

> 'We do not find obvious evidence of life or mind in so-called inert matter, and we naturally study them most easily where they are most completely manifested; but if the scientific point of view is correct, we shall ultimately find them, at least in rudimentary forms, all through the universe. . . . Now, if the co-operation of some thousands of millions of cells in our brain can produce our consciousness, the idea becomes vastly more plausible that the co-operation of humanity, or some sections of it, may determine what Comte calls 'a Great 'Being''.'

The second part of this quotation becomes of special significance in relation to Teilhard's final conclusions at the end of *The Phenomenon of Man*.

The second unconventional and original conception which Teilhard adumbrates in this chapter concerns Energy. Nothing is more familiar to us than spiritual energy; upon the objective reality of which, the entire structure of Ethics, and much else, rests. But nothing is more baffling scientifically.

> 'It would be very convenient if we could follow Science in ignoring the inescapable coherence of spiritual and material energy. Fortunately (or unfortunately), bound as we are by the logic of an Inwardness of things as well as their Outwardness, this is impossible. We must go forward' (p. 59).

Teilhard then goes on to point out that material energy is, for Man, a prerequisite of spiritual energy. 'In order to think, it is necessary to eat'. He deduces that, in the final analysis, there is probably only one single energy in the world; but a *direct* transformation of the one apparent sort into the other must be excluded; such an explanation is impossibly superficial. The essence of his own, admittedly tentative, solution is as follows:

'Essentially, all energy is, we will admit, of a spiritual ('psychique') nature. But in each particular element, we shall add, this fundamental energy is divided into two distinct components: a *tangential energy*, which classes that element among all the elements of the same order as itself in the Universe (i.e. of the same complexity and centricity); and a *radial energy*, which draws it on towards an ever more complex state, centred towards the future' (p. 62).

Upon this question of energy, which inevitably involves him in the problem of entropy, Teilhard does not, at this point, reach any final conclusions.

The comment made by Sir Julian Huxley, in his Introduction, is as follows:

'He seeks to link the evolution of mind with the concept of energy. If I understand him aright, he envisages two forms of energy, or perhaps two modes in which it is manifested— energy in the physicists' sense, measurable or calcuable by physical methods, and 'psychic energy' which increases with the complexity of organised units (we certainly need some new terms in this field: perhaps *neurergy* and *psychergy* would serve). This view admittedly involves speculation of great intellectual boldness, but the speculation is extrapolated from a massive array of fact, and is disciplined by logic. It is, if you like, visionary: but it is the product of a comprehensive and coherent vision' (Introduction p. 16).

The third chapter of the section *Before Life* is devoted to a description of the ever growing complexity of molecular structures on the surface of the as yet lifeless Earth. Teilhard uses the technical word 'polymerisation', though, as he explains, in a sense wider than the strictly chemical one. This process, although only a hypothesis for which no evidence survives (which is equally true of all that happened for several thousand millennia), was the indispensable prerequisite for the appearance of Life.

The substance of most of the section *Life* can be summarised briefly. The broad outline of it is generally familiar; and, fascinating though it is, there is little that is Teilhard's contribution, except the expressive term *Biosphere*, and its important connotation —the *unity* of Life. The process of its emergence ran from the mega-molecule to the macro-molecule, to the cell which was a living organism. (The quite recent discovery of viruses caused Teilhard to observe that we may not know as much as we thought of the stages of this process.) It almost certainly took place in the waters of the tepid ocean that covered the entire Earth; and it took place once for all. There is no evidence that it takes place now; and man has so far failed entirely to reproduce it in the laboratory. Teilhard points out that in the cell there appears 'the stuff of the Universe, raised to a higher degree of complexity . . . and at the same time to a higher degree of Inwardness' (p. 89). How to explain 'a higher degree of Inwardness' is, he confesses, difficult; he surmounts the difficulty by an elegant analogy: 'A circle may increase the order of its symmetry by becoming a sphere' (p. 91).

The fact that protoplasm was formed once, and once only, has for Teilhard great significance. For the following reasons:

(i) It provides a reason for the profound organic similarity of all living things, from Bacteria to Man.

(ii) By separating the phenomenon of life from all periodical and secondary terrestrial events, and making it one of the chief landmarks in the sidereal evolution of the globe, it gives us a truer sense of values and a new perspective.

(iii) By linking the origin of organised bodies to a chemical transformation unique in terrestrial history, it inclines us to regard the energy contained in the living layer of our planet as developing from, and within, a kind of closed 'quantum', defined by the amplitude of this primordial emission (p. 107).

It would be little to my purpose, and take disproportionate space, to summarise in any detail the remainder of Teilhard's second Section, in which he describes at some length the ramification of the Tree of Life. In the third chapter of it, we are upon the threshold of something new. He sums up all that has gone before as first the shifting of the axis of Geogenesis (in the 'Lithosphere') so that it prolonged itself in Biogenesis (in the 'Biosphere'); henceforth it will express itself definitively in

Psychogenesis (i.e. in the 'Noosphere') (p. 161), which brings us to the third Section *Thought*.

Here, almost at the beginning, he asks a dramatic question:

'Between the latest strata of the Pliocene, from which Man is absent, and the following level, where the geologist is struck dumb with amazement at recognizing the first chipped flints, what happened? And what is the real dimension of this leap?' (p. 180).

The reply is that a creature has appeared who has taken the first 'Step to Reflection'. This is Man; and Man's uniqueness lies primarily in this: 'non plus seulement connaître—mais se connaître; non plus seulement savoir, mais savoir que l'on sait' (no translation is wholly satisfactory. The basic meaning is: 'No longer merely to have knowledge, but to have knowledge of oneself. No longer merely to know, but to know that one knows.' The animal, Teilhard says, admittedly knows. But it is quite certain that it cannot know that it knows. If it did, the history of the world would have been quite different. Thus began the process for which Teilhard invented the word 'hominization'. We are now upon the threshold of the Noosphere.

The earliest stages of Man's unwritten history were Teilhard's speciality as an anthropologist. He describes what we know, or can reasonably conjecture, of the process that turned the Anthropoid into the Hominid; and recounts the very fragmentary chapters known to us of the history of the Hominids, down to Neanderthaler. And then, suddenly, at the end of the last Ice Age, from Europe to China, we find Homo Sapiens. And he is ourselves. Of what went on in the mind of Neanderthaler, our distant cousin, we have no idea. Far different is it with Homo Sapiens.

'But in the age of the reindeer, with Homo Sapiens, Thought, finally liberated, explodes in all its warmth on the walls of the caves. In their own persons, the new comers brought Art—an art still naturalistic but prodigiously accomplished'. (p. 224)

Anyone who has seen Lascaux or Pèche Merle will agree.

At this point, Teilhard's whole emphasis shifts. The hominization which produced Man is accomplished. The interest now turns to the further hominization of itself which Humanity is still in process of carrying out, the final stages of which provide the matter for Teilhard's most original speculation. This process had to become global before getting into full and effective operation. Indeed, it is part of his thesis that this 'folding in upon itself' ('enroulement sur soi-même') has still very much further to go before Humanity achieves all its potential. In its first, Neolithic, stages, the process did not, as a global phenomenon, get very far.

'We can recognise five such foci, in a more or less distant past: Central America, with its Maya civilisation; the South Seas, with their Polynesian civilisation; the basin of the Yellow River, with the Chinese; the valleys of the Ganges and the Indus, with the civilisations of India; and finally the Nile and Mesopotamia, with Egypt and Sumeria'. (p. 232).

For geographical reasons, Maya and Polynesia advanced no further. For the same reason, perhaps with a psychological one added, China did not either. It must be remembered that Teilhard had spent a quarter of a century in China when he wrote:

'Until yesterday, this gigantic country represented, still living beneath our eyes, a scarcely modified fragment of the world, as it may have been ten thousand years ago'. As for India, its philosophical cast of mind stood in the way of further development.

'When phenomena were regarded as illusion (Maya), and their inter-relations as a chain (Karma), what was left to these doctrines for the animation and direction of human evolution?' (p. 234). Hence it remained to the civilisations of the Euphrates, the Nile and the Mediterranean, to head human advance. The successive downfall of various parts did not break the rising spiral of Life. 'Susa, Memphis, Athens may perish. An ever more fully organised consciousness of the Universe is passed on from hand to hand; and its brightness increases'. It is in the human terms which have, in the last six thousand years, been formulated around the Mediterranean, that the entire modern world conceives its hopes and its problems. This human solidarity is the condition for remaining human.

The last chapter of Teilhard's third Section is entitled 'The Modern Earth'. Man, he says, has always thought himself to be

at a turning point in history; since the end of the eighteenth
century there has indeed been, in the West, a decisive change of
course. The essence of this change is to be found in a new
intuition, an awakening, in other words, which has totally
modified the physiognómy of the Universe in which we were
moving. Unless I am mistaken, this modification, says Teilhard,
'consists in our having become conscious of the movement which
carries us along; which has caused us to perceive the redoubtable
problems set us by the reflective exercise of the human Effort'
(p. 238).

What Teilhard calls this 'noogenesis' began 'when the walls
of Space were shaken by the Renaissance, and then, from Buffon
onwards, both the floor and the ceiling of Time became mobile'
(p. 240). . . . It was not until well into the nineteenth century,
still under the influence of biology, that there finally began to
dawn the light which reveals the *irreversible coherence* of all that
exists (p. 241). . . . What constitutes and classifies *modern* man (and
in this sense, a host of our contemporaries are not yet modern)
is to have become capable of seeing, not only in terms of Space,
not only in terms of Time, but in those of Duration; or—
which comes to the same thing—in terms of biological Space-
Time, and finding himself, moreover, incapable of seeing anything
in other terms, including himself' (p. 243). Although at first,
scientists did not envisage themselves as caught in its current:

'Evolution, whether we like it or not, is now extending to the
spiritual zones of the world, thus transferring to the spiritual
structures raised by Life, not only the stuff, but the cosmic
'primacy' hitherto reserved by Science for the involved whirl-
winds of the old "ether" ' (p. 244). Man has discovered that, in
Julian Huxley's cogent phrase, he is *nothing else than Evolution
become conscious of itself.*

What, for Teilhard, gives this Process supreme significance is
that it did not start with us. 'The wave which we feel passing
was not formed within us ourselves. It reaches us from very far
away—it started at the same time as the light from the first stars.
It reaches us after having created everything in its passage. The
spirit which seeks and conquers is the lasting soul of Evolution.
. . . Man, not the centre of the Universe, as we naively used to
think, but, which is far fairer, Man the upward flying arrow of the
grand biological synthesis; Man, constituting in himself alone,

the latest born, the freshest, the most complex, the most subtle of the successive layers of Life' (pp. 248–9).

The writer of *Ecclesiastes* said long ago that 'He that increaseth knowledge increaseth sorrow'. For having grown to the knowledge that he is Evolution become conscious of itself, Man has to pay a price, which Teilhard describes thus: 'At the root of the modern world's disquiet lies the uncertainty, and the ignorance of how to emerge from that uncertainty, whether there is an outcome—the right outcome—to Evolution' (p. 254) and for Teilhard there can be only one answer: either Man takes up the challenge, or else he deliberately refuses it. In either case, the issue is inevitable: 'Either Nature presents a closed door to our demands for a future. In which case, Thought, the fruit of millions of years of effort, is suffocated, still-born, in an absurd Universe which produces its own abortion. Or there is an opening, for the super-soul above our souls; but this opening, for us to consent to take it, must be without restriction into limitless spaces of the spirit, within a Universe which we can trust with all our heart and soul' (p. 258).

His final section is devoted to *The Future of Life* (his own word, 'La Survie' is used by him rather in the sense of 'The super-Life,' than of 'survival', which is the official translation). In the first chapter he draws a picture of the Noosphere continually folding in upon itself and attaining an ever increasing concentration of collective consciousness. It is the 'natural culmination of an organic process of organisation which has never varied since the distant ages when our planet was young' (p. 270). To this everything has contributed, from the fact that the earth is spherical, and Man's zoological uniqueness in having covered the entire planet with 'a single organised membrane', to the contemporary strengthening of that membrane by his ever quickening means of communication. A number of striking terms are used in the description: 'A new Phylogenesis'; 'mega-Synthesis'; 'human Planetisation'. The result, according to Teilhard, is that: 'Man can expect no evolutionary future except by association with other men' (p. 273). 'The Biosphere hitherto formed one assembly of divergent lines, free at their extremities. Beneath the effect of Reflection, and of the infolding which this produces, the chains close; and the Noosphere tends to become one single closed system—in which each element for itself sees, feels, desires, suffers the same things as all the others at the same time' (p. 279).

As far as my own objective is concerned, this exposition of *Le Phénomène humain* could here be brought to an end. My purpose in these pages has been to illustrate the development of Man's conception of Cosmic Process. In Teilhard de Chardin, that has reached the furthest limit. Viewing the human scene in the mid-twentieth century, he sees it as not only Evolution in full spate, and conscious of itself, but as irretrievably and irreversibly committed to evermore complex and self-accelerating evolution. This evolution, within the Noosphere itself, he envisages as henceforth exosomatic rather than genetic.[1] In these two final chapters of the book, 'The hyper-Personal' and 'The final World', Teilhard is perhaps at his most personal and characteristic. It was for the sake of expressing this ultimate vision that the whole remarkable book was written. He claims that all he has seen and shown us must inevitably culminate in just this vision. In this he may have been mistaken. Not everyone is agreed that the future must inevitably be what he prophesies it to be. One perfectly sound reason—there are others—is that he has perhaps left out of his analysis one factor of the greatest importance. I should myself say that this factor was the origin, nature and consequence of Evil. But it would be most unsatisfactory, from every point of view, as well as entirely unjust to one of the most remarkable authors of our time, to withhold his final dénouement. The essence of it, therefore, now follows. But it is only the essence, and I give but an outline. To see the picture in the detail in which he paints it, the reader must go to Teilhard himself.

In the chapter 'The hyper-Personal', Teilhard attempts to deal with an obvious and most urgent danger. 'Because it contains and engenders consciousness, Space-Time is necessarily of a convergent nature. Because its enormous layers, followed in

---

[1]As witness the following passage (p. 309):
'Depuis que l'Homme est apparu, la pression évolutive semble être tombée dans toutes les branches non humaines de l'Arbre de la Vie. Et maintenant qu'à l'Homme devenu adulte s'est ouvert le champ des transformations mentales et sociales, les corps ne changent plus appréciablement—ils n'ont plus à changer dans la branche humaine; ou s'ils changent encore, ce ne sera plus que sous notre industrieux contrôle. Il se peut que, dans ses capacités et sa pénétration individuelles notre cerveau ait atteint ses limites organiques. Mais le mouvement ne s'arrête pas pour autant. De l'Occident à l'Orient, l'Évolution est désormais occupée ailleurs, dans un domaine plus riche et plus complexe, à construire avec tous les esprits mis ensemble, l'*Esprit*.'

the right direction, must, somewhere in the future, fold together into a point—let us call it *Omega*—which fuses and brings them into an integral consummation in itself' (p. 288). But if that is all, the final result of the coming into existence of the Noosphere would be the disappearance of the personality, the entity capable of 'noein'—to think. That capacity, as Descartes pointed out, is the surest proof of individual man's existence. According to Teilhard himself, it was that which produced the Noosphere.

This dilemma Teilhard seeks to solve by an intricate hypothesis of the 'centricity' of personality; which leads to the assertion that: 'By its structure, considered in its final principle, Omega can only be a distinct Centre radiating at the heart of a system of centres' (p. 292). The proof of this 'centricity' of personality Teilhard finds in the ultimate nature of Love; which draws together, and fuses in one, two entities which yet retain their personalities.

The third chapter, 'The final World', begins with some consideration of the inevitable 'death of our planet'. But Teilhard dismisses all the apocalyptic prognostications, such as collision with another heavenly body, as unlikely; and points out that, failing a sudden premature end, Humanity is likely to have before it several hundred million years. This means: 'An advance ever higher into the Improbable out of which we have come. If we wish to picture to ourselves the End of the World, it is in this direction that we must extrapolate Man and Hominization' (p. 307).

Three obvious lines of advance can already be foreseen. Further scientific research in many directions, with resources liberated from their present misuse for political purposes (e.g. armaments); the progressively greater application of Man's increasing knowledge to an improvement of his race (e.g. eugenics); and the convergence of Science and Religion. For two centuries they have done battle, neither succeeding in defeating its adversary— for the simple reason that it is the same life that animates both. 'Religion and Science: two faces, or linked phases, of one single complete act of knowledge; the only one which can embrace the past and the future of Evolution, to contemplate, measure and complete them' (p. 317).

When he comes to consider the final phase ('Le Terme'), Teilhard glances at, and dismisses as improbable, a leap by Humanity beyond this planet into other worlds. He is left with a continually increasing Noogenesis on Earth; ending in the final, integral infolding of the Noosphere itself, when it has reached the limits of complexity and 'centricity'. And then: 'The end of the world. The overthrow of equilibrium; the detaching of the Mind ('Esprit'), now perfected, from its Matrix in Matter, so that it shall henceforth rest with all its weight upon God-Omega' (p. 320). And here, at the very end of his book, Teilhard suddenly admits the possibility of a dualism which he has denied, or rather totally ignored, all through. 'Will Man seek to fulfil himself collectively upon himself? Or personally upon a greater than himself? Will he refuse or accept Omega?' (p. 321). In any case the planet Earth will die, physically worn-out. Even if the worst comes to the worst, there will be 'a rending of the Noosphere, divided upon the form which its unity should assume; and simultaneously, giving full significance and value to the event, there will be a liberation of that portion of the Universe which, across Time, Space and Evil, will have succeeded in carrying its own synthesis, with toil and labour, to the end' (p.322). With this, *Le Phénomène humain*, except for a few summarising and valedictory sentences, concludes.

In the fourteen years since it appeared, there have followed nine other volumes of writings from Teilhard's pen, the larger part of which he had not himself prepared for publication. Many of his letters have also been published; and there is also material still unpublished. In these years there has grown up, and there is still growing, a considerable literature, in at least four languages, around Teilhard, his life, scientific achievements, merits, faults and so-called heresies. Much of it is controversial, sometimes to the point of being ludicrous. None of these concerns my theme; which has been solely the exposition of *Le Phénomène humain* as the culmination, so far, of Man's conception of Cosmic Process.

In conclusion, I am going to claim the author's privilege of making my own small criticisms of this remarkable book. To say that it is not to claim for them any originality; the cataract of denunciation that has descended upon Teilhard, chiefly from the theologians of his own church, must contain every conceivable charge; but nothing of what I have to say has been taken from that source. Moreover, what I have to say is not based upon the whole corpus of Teilhard's writings, and concerns nothing except *Le Phénomène humain*.

At the end of the book, Teilhard tacks on what are virtually two appendices, although only the second is so called. The first, which he calls an Epilogue, is entitled 'The Christian Phenomenon'. In this, he attempts to integrate Christianity into the whole metaphysic of the book. Christ, he says, 'by a personal act of communion and sublimation integrates into himself the total spiritual energy ("psychisme") of the Earth' (p. 327). And a little later: 'If the world is convergent, and if Christ occupies its centre, then the Christogenesis of St. Paul and St. John is nothing other, and nothing less, than the prolongation, at once expected and unhoped-for, in which, as far as our experience goes, Cosmogenesis culminates' (p. 331). It needs no very learned theologian to point out that no such view can be based upon the Fourth Gospel; which begins thus: 'In the beginning was the Word, and the Word was with God and the Word was God. . . . All things were made by him, and without him was not anything made that was made.' The Greek ($\pi\acute{\alpha}\nu\tau\alpha$ $\delta\iota'$ $\alpha\mathring{v}\tau o\mathring{v}$ $\mathring{\epsilon}\gamma\acute{\epsilon}\nu\epsilon\tau o$) leaves no possible doubt that the Logos was, if not the cause, at least the precondition, of the act of creation. In such terms, therefore, Christogenesis cannot be called the prolongation or culmination of Cosmogenesis.[1]

The fact, of course, is that Teilhard would have been much better advised not to attempt to bring Christianity into Le Phénomène humain at all. To make the attempt was to invite what he got: the condemnation both of his fellow Christians and of his fellow scientists. The first rejected his scientific heresies, and the second his religious preconceptions. Teilhard elsewhere wrote much that is both eloquent and moving about the Master to whose service he had vowed his life. But the attempt to integrate Christianity, after more than 300 pages, into what he claimed to be a scientific work, and what is certainly a metaphysical one, was foredoomed to failure.

The underlying reason for this failure is perhaps to be seen in his Appendix on 'The place and part of Evil in an evolving world'. Here again, so vast and so important a subject cannot be dismissed in three pages of Appendix. In this case, it should surely have formed part of his theme from the beginning. Conscious of this criticism, Teilhard added an appendix, in which, in

---

[1] The ninth volume of the collected works is entitled *Science et Christ*. It is to this that anyone wishing to acquaint himself with Teilhard's views upon the subject should first go.

effect, he says that, though he has said nothing about Evil in his book, he has taken it for granted. 'What I did not say, I supposed would still be perceived. And it would therefore have been a total misunderstanding of the vision here proposed to seek in it a sort of human idyll in place of the cosmic drama which I have wished to evoke'(p. 345). He enumerates various forms of Evil, and more or less intimates that in an evolving world they are inevitable. But he admits that this is an inadequate explanation. To the mind that regards the world by a light other than that of pure Science, 'Does not Evil here and now spread about the world, betray a certain *excess*, inexplicable to our reason if, *to the normal effect of Evolution*, there be not superadded the *extraordinary effect* of some primordial catastrophe or deviation? Upon this matter I honestly do not feel able, nor would this be the place, to take up a position' (p. 347-8).

The tremendous and impressive picture which *Le Phénomène humain* paints is in two dimensions: the physical and the metaphysical. But Humanity can only be adequately represented in three dimensions. One of these Teilhard has omitted. That is the moral. It is fundamentally for that reason that his Epilogue on Christianity and his Appendix on Evil are so unsatisfactory and inadequate. He attempts, in his metaphysical terms, to explain the Incarnation. What he does not, and in those terms cannot, attempt to explain is the Crucifixion. And it is by the Crucifixion that there is achieved Redemption.

'This is a faithful saying, and worthy of all acceptation, that Christ Jesus came into the world to save sinners.'

EPILOGUE

When he first received the typescript of this book, my publisher, being a prudent man, sent it to a 'fairly young theologian', for an opinion. He later sent me the opinion, which I found most interesting and very helpful; and as a result of it I partly rewrote the third chapter. Here is one paragraph; which I quote without being able to make a personal acknowledgement; since the whole transaction was entirely anonymous, and I have no idea of the identity of my helpful critic:

'I would have liked to see more than a statement of the inappropriateness of dragging Christ into *Le Phénomène humain*. That is on the face of it a rather obvious criticism, but the fact is that Christ was vitally important to Teilhard. Mr. Rutland says that Teilhard's vision is physical and metaphysical, but not moral, and Christianity is supremely moral. But a process whose goal is love seems to me the foundation of all morality. Mr. Rutland is clearly a Christian, and cares about Cosmic Process—could he not give the book some personal conclusion, which it lacks—by trying to say what, for him, the growing consciousness of Process adds up to?'

In this request he is entirely right; and in the few pages that follow I have attempted to meet it. But first I deal with his remarks about the conclusion of my fourth chapter.

It is precisely because Christ *was* vitally important to Teilhard that I pointed out and regretted the brevity and inadequacy of the attempt to integrate Christianity into *Le Phénomène humain* only at the end of three hundred pages. Rather than this, it seemed to me, it would have been preferable not to make the attempt at all. There is, in the whole book, no reference to God (except the arguably ambiguous one near the end, where the culmination of the Cosmic Process on earth is called 'God-Omega').

Anyone who desires the uplifting and ennobling experience of reading Teilhard on Christ and God should go to *Le Milieu divin*.[1] The whole scope of *Le Phénomène humain*, its conception

[1] 'Le progrès de l'univers, et spécialement de l'univers humain, n'est pas une concurrence faite à Dieu, ni une déperdition vaine des energies que nous lui devons. Plus l'homme sera grand, plus l'Humanité sera unie, consciente et maîtresse de sa force—plus aussi la création sera belle, plus l'adoration sera parfaite, plus le Christ trouvera, pour des extensions mystiques, un corps digne de résurrection.' *Le Milieu divin*, p. 200.

and, until the last few pages, its execution are, as I said, devoted to the physical and the metaphysical. Which brings me to the point that 'Christianity is supremely moral'. My critic is, of course, right in recognising me to be a Christian. He would surely agree with me that the essence of Christianity is a moral one, in the sense that it is concerned with Good and Evil. For the Christian, there stands at the heart of man's universe the Cross of Christ; and the significance of that Cross (as I thought my final quotation from St. Paul made clear) is victory over Evil.

Now the whole question of Evil nowhere arises in *Le Phénomène humain* until we reach the insignificant Appendix; where we are told that it is probably an inevitable by-product of an evolving Universe; but that this, as Teilhard acknowledges, is an inadequate explanation of a phenomenon 'here and now spread about the world'. Surely my critic, especially as he is a theologian, needs no further explanation, or justification, of the opinion that Christianity cannot be discussed on such premises. He will know, if he has read any Teilhardiana, that I am by no means alone in holding that opinion. I reached it when I read *Le Phénomène humain* on its first appearance, long before I read any Teilhard criticism.

I come now to the personal statement for which my critic asked. This, I would emphasise, is not an *apologia pro vita mea*; still less is it a *defensio fidei*. It is an account, in the form of a pocket intellectual autobiography, of the history of my own interest in Cosmic Process, and what it has done for me. Certain quotations which I give in the course of it, two of them long and famous ones, should be illuminating.

In the first place, it seems to me hardly possible for any highly educated man or woman at the present day, acquainted with the evidence that I have tried to set forth, to deny the existence of Cosmic Process. Until quite recently it was, in some states of the United States of America, an offence punishable by dismissal and prosecution, to 'teach' Evolution in a state school. I believe I am correct in saying that this position has now been overturned by a decision of the United States Supreme Court. The attitude of mind upon which it was based will be familiar to anyone familiar with the controversies which raged in England in the eighteen-sixties and seventies, following the publication of *The Origin of Species*. To us in England, these are now chiefly of historical interest. It remains true that, as I have tried to show, the whole mentality of modern Western man is largely the result of the growth of the idea of Cosmic Process. It has been of the greatest value to me, in the understanding of that mentality, and of the world in which I have lived, to have been familiar with its sources and its history. But much more than that; it has immeasurably enlarged all my own horizons. To these I now turn.

To deal in the first place with something that I have but briefly mentioned. The first and most catastrophic (if one may so phrase it) 'Death of God' took place in Western Europe in the second half of the nineteenth century. It was the direct result of the investigation of Cosmic Process, by the science of the period, using the techniques then available, and the hypotheses constructed upon the data so provided. What logically resulted is what used to be known (though the eighteenth century term is no longer fashionable) as 'naturalism'. It was the conception of the Universe as a mechanism. To illustrate the results of such a conception upon human thought one quotation will be sufficient. Here is the description of this state of mind written by Arthur James Balfour, that remarkable, and, in our day, inconceivable combination of thinker and politician, who became Prime Minister of Great Britain in 1902:

'Man, so far as natural science by itself is able to teach us, is no longer . . . the Heaven descended heir of all the ages. His very existence is accidental, his history a brief and transitory episode in the life of one of the meanest of the planets. Of the combination of causes which first converted a dead organic compound into the living progenitors of humanity, science, indeed, as yet knows nothing. It is enough that from such beginnings, famine, disease and mutual slaughter, fit nurses of the future lords of creation, has gradually evolved, after infinite travail, a race with conscience enough to feel that it is vile, and intelligence enough to know that it is insignificant.

'We survey the past, and see that its history is of blood and tears, of helpless blundering, of wild revolt, of stupid acquiescence, of empty aspirations. We sound the future, and learn that after a period, long compared with the individual life, but short indeed compared with the divisions of time open to our investigation, the energies of our system will decay, the glory of the sun will be dimmed, and the earth, tideless and inert, will no longer tolerate the race which has for a moment disturbed its solitude. Man will go down into the pit, and all his thoughts will perish. The uneasy consciousness, which in this obscure corner has for a brief space broken the contented silence of the Universe, will be at rest. Matter will know itself no longer. Imperishable monuments and immortal deeds, death itself and love stronger than death, will be as though they had never been. Nor will anything that is be better or be worse for all that the labour, genius, devotion and suffering of man have striven through countless generations to effect'[1].

What a piece of prose! And what a nightmare it describes! If that is the conclusion to which the Cosmic Process led, no wonder that Thomas Henry Huxley asserted in his famous Romanes lecture that Man's duty was to combat it. Nevertheless, strange as it may seem, this comfortless, draughty structure of a mechanistic universe, built of the atoms which they took to be its ultimate bricks, seems to have provided an acceptable—even a welcome—habitation for a certain type of mind. The classic example is probably to be found in Haeckel's provocative manifesto, the English translation of which, under the title *The Riddle of the Universe*, appeared in 1900. Haeckel, who had in his day been a considerable scientist, here donned the mantle of the prophet, ascended into the pulpit, and announced that the religion of the twentieth century will be 'scientific monism'. I remember how, in my youth, a number of elderly atheists, who feared that I might be enticed into Holy Orders (than which, for them, there was no worse calamity), told me much the same thing, and how lucky I was to be going to live in it. Well, I have lived in it; and I have seen their house of cards collapse. It would be interesting to see Haeckel trying to reconstruct it seventy years later. The vision of a German professor (irresistibly associated in my mind with Teufelsdröck), constructing with the Principle of Indeterminacy and the Quantum physics of the nineteen-sixties, a 'scientific religion', is to me irresistibly comic, if not pathetic.

But to those who were confronted with the materialism of seventy years ago, and took the scientists proclaiming it at their own valuation, it was anything but comic. It was intolerable. As there are limits to the physical agony which the body can endure, beyond which lies death, so there are limits to the agony

[1] *The Foundations of Belief* (1895), p. 30–31.

I

of the human imagination, beyond which lies the extinction of all that differentiates man from animals. In A. J. Balfour's description, that limit has been reached. When Job reached his nadir, his wife told him to curse God and die. Homo Sapiens, deprived of faith as A. J. Balfour saw him in 1891, could not even do that. For there was no God to curse. But the resources of the human spirit are not so circumscribed. It had conceived materialism, which it found to be unbearable. It conceived vitalism. If the science of the nineteenth century had removed a transcendent God from the Universe, it now substituted an immanent God within the Universe; a living force which *was* the Universe; a Vital Urge which impelled an evolutionary Cosmic Process. The best description of this is perhaps to be found in one of the most eloquent passages in that eloquent book, Henri Bergson's *L'Evolution créatrice* (1907). Here is what Bergson wrote of the combined possibilities of consciousness and intuition:

'Mais une telle doctrine ne facilite pas seulement la spéculation. Elle nous donne aussi plus de force pour agir et pour vivre. Car, avec elle, nous ne nous sentons plus isolés dans l'humanité, l'humanité ne nous semble pas non plus isolée dans la nature qu'elle domine. Comme le plus petit grain de poussière est solidaire de notre système solaire tout entier, entraîné avec lui dans ce mouvement indivisé de descente qui est la matérialité même, ainsi tous les êtres organisés, du plus humble au plus élevé, depuis les premières origines de la vie jusqu'au temps où nous sommes, et dans tous les lieux comme dans tous les temps, ne font que rendre sensible aux yeux une impulsion unique, inverse du mouvement de la matière, et en elle-même, indivisible. Tous les vivants se tiennent, et tous cèdent à la même formidable poussée. L'animal prend son point d'appui sur la planète, l'homme chevauche sur l'animalité, et l'humanité entière, dans l'espace et dans le temps, est une immense armée qui galope à côté de chacun de nous, dans une charge entraînante capable de culbuter toutes les résistances et de franchir bien des obstacles, même peut-être la mort'[1].

Magnificent! That is a heady brew for young men to read. We students of the generations immediately after the 1914–18 war did read it. One of the most gifted of my friends, who had had too

[1] *L'Evolution créatrice*, end of ch. 3.

Vitalism, opponent of materialism, held
lacking in personal and moral elements.

EPILOGUE   113

much conventional religion injudiciously foisted upon him as a
child, is something of a Bergsonian to this day. For me, Bergson's
Universe lacked two elements which were to my mind indispensable: the personal and the moral. His galloping host of all living
things, launched upon a charge capable of overthrowing all
resistance, and perhaps overcoming death itself, was of no help
to me when, in my twenty-first year, I learnt for the first time
what it meant for death to take from me someone whom I loved.

When I took my first degree, I had become a communicant
member of the Christian Church. So far from removing my
speculative intellectual interest in the nature of causation in the
Universe, this very greatly increased it. Not only had I now a
strong personal commitment. I had a secure base upon an
unshakeable terra firma from which to carry out my explorations.

The directions into which they took me appear to some extent
in the book on Swinburne which I published in 1931[1]. Much
more directly, they are the subject of a poem which the same
publisher produced for me two years later. This is entitled
Creation, has for its epigraph a quotation from the Prolog im
Himmel, and consists of a series of narratives by the archangels
Michael, Raphael, Gabriel and Azrael. Michael expounds, in
Miltonic manner, the theory of the origin of the Solar System
then being put forward by Jeans. Raphael and Gabriel recount
the growth of what correspond pretty closely to Teilhard's biosphere and noosphere (this was twenty-two years before *Le
Phénomène humain* appeared). Here are two stanzas from Raphael:

> I well remember how I walked beside
> Triassic waters; by the rising tide
>   Were all the seaweed islands landward drawn;
> When suddenly I heard a sound of flight,
> Saw bony membranes stretched in the half-light,
>   Pterodactylic wings against the dawn.

> And a great clamour and crying came down the wind
> From that half bird-like, half reptilian kind,
>   Rising above the palms with one accord.
> In many a stately fane have I heard sung
> What they tried sing; never more truly rung
>   'Laudate Dominum—O praise the Lord!'

[1] Op. cit.

This particularly appealed to C. S. Lewis; who was to become one of my most valued friends, and the godfather of my elder son. He wrote to me: 'A choir of pterodactyls! Glory, what a conception!'

Gabriel's narrative illustrates clearly how I myself regarded, and still regard, certain rationalist attitudes:

> This human thing which Wisdom brought to birth
> In the primeval forests with the ape,
> Hath with the passing years, although his shape
> Scarcely hath changed, developed mind to think
> A little, and a very little to know.
> Because his lips have tasted at the brink
> One drop from the deep cup of knowledge, lo
> He crieth 'I am crown of all things. Go,
> 'See if thou find another thing like me
> 'In depths of space beyond eternity.
> 'My human mind hath fathomed the abyss;
> 'And the end of dreams anthropomorphic this—
> 'No God at all nor mind nor purpose is'.

How much my concern with emergent creation was, unlike Teilhard's noosphere, directed towards moral questions rather than towards mere cerebral intelligence, the following extract from Gabriel's résumé of human history will show (his quotation is a translation of *Oedipus Rex*, 845, et seq.):

> Ye know the play played in past centuries
> Beneath the shadow of the Acropolis,
> A fearful tale of incest and of blood
> Wrought by the will of primitive deities (these
> Were but in the primitive mind), yet Sophocles
> In all that welter of evil knew the good.
> 'O might I have in every word and deed
> 'That innocence' (ye heard the chorus plead)
> 'Whereof the laws are holy, and in the sky
> 'Begotten, not brought forth of mortality,
> 'Nor ever of oblivion lulled to sleep'
> (Heard ye the echo answering from the deep
> Of stellar space and night and ultimate cold?)
> 'Mighty in these is God and grows not old.'

I have spoken of my dissatisfaction with vitalism, in the 1920s. In passing, I may mention the same dissatisfaction expressed by a great man, whom we generally think of as a man of action rather than contemplation, at that very time. General, afterwards Field Marshal, Jan Smuts published, in 1928, a notable book entitled *Holism*. This puts forward an alternative hypothesis to vitalism, which it would here be inappropriate to discuss. But in the twenty years after *L'Evolution créatice*, the whole question was receiving the attention of professional philosophers. The most notable of the English ones are mentioned in my Introduction, and its notes. From one of them I will here quote. Although now probably only familiar to students of philosophy, Samuel Alexander's *Space, Time and Deity* (1916) shows as clearly as Bergson, but from an altogether different angle, how the nineteenth century Theory of Evolution, mostly based upon contemporary physics and biology, was widening and deepening into the twentieth century's conception of Cosmic Process; which took into account many other matters, unknown to the nineteenth century, such as anthropology and psychology. Alexander's essential theme, if the essence of two large closely reasoned volumes can be stated in a few words, is this:

The ultimate, in the sense of original, creative energy is the Universe of Space-Time itself (beyond which it is useless, and probably meaningless, for our analysis to attempt to penetrate). The Universe of Space-Time has created Consciousness. It is in process of creating Deity. As Consciousness is above, and different in kind and not only in degree from, all that preceded it, so Deity is above, and different from, though not alien to, Consciousness. Here is a passage from the concluding section:

'When we think of God as that to which all things owe their existence, we are reversing the order of fact and are regarding the Universe of Space-Time, which does create all things, in the light of its highest empirical quality, which is not first but last in the order of generation. The notion of a creator God is a hybrid blending of the creative Space-Time with the created Deity. It searches for Deity by a backward instead of a forward view. Accordingly, in its relation to conduct, religion does not so much command us to perform our duties with the consciousness that they are commands of God, as rather it is religion to do our duty with the consciousness of helping to create his Deity'[1].

As appeared in connection with Teilhard de Chardin and his Appendix to *Le Phénomène humain*, possibly the greatest single problem of religion is the question of Evil; and more especially the problem of suffering, and what Dr. Robinson calls 'prevenient intention'. It may be remarked in passing that Samuel Alexander attempted to provide a morally and intellectually acceptable escape from this dilemma. He has no difficulty in showing how, on his theory of the progressive emergence of Deity created by Space-Time, no problem of prevenient intention arises. These matters were a profound preoccupation to Thomas Hardy for most of his long life, as I have tried to show in my study of him. The very tentative solution which he reached is to be seen in the *Dynasts*. I can only say that for me personally, the intellectual difficulties of any such solution are at least equal to the moral difficulty of the problem which it attempts to solve.

The conclusion of the whole matter (to use the language of *Ecclesiastes*) must be to try and sum up what a growing consciousness of Cosmic Process adds up to, for me personally here and now; and also what it does not. This can perhaps best be achieved by a short dialogue between me and an imaginary, rather simple-minded, questioner.

Q. As you say you are a Christian, surely you know, and have for many years known, all the answers to all the questions about God. Is not all this theorising about Cosmic Process simply an intellectual diversion, a sort of metaphysical five-finger exercise? Does it really make any significant difference to you personally?

I. Is that your only question? Because, if you have others, I would like my final answer to be to that one.

Q. Well, yes; there are all the big questions, to which this idea of Cosmic Process must obviously make a difference. What does it all mean? Did God start the Universe? Is he still transcendent to it, or must we think of him now as partly or wholly immanent within it? And if we are to take seriously this theory of Deity emerging from the Universe of Space-Time, how did that Universe start? And what about the people at Cambridge,

---

[1] *Space, Time and Deity*, vol. 2, p. 399.

who say that the Universe never had a start? And what about the people at Oxford, who say that, even if anybody does know anything, (which nobody knows), nobody else can know it; because you cannot say what you know, or know what you say—I forget which.

I. If you'd ever taught at Oxford, you would not let trifles like that worry you. As to Cambridge, I never pretended to understand mathematics. But there are people at Manchester who have a radio telescope, with which they study quasars; and these, they say, prove that the Universe did have a start. Anyhow, you aren't asking me much, are you? I am reminded of A. A. Milne's poem:

> Elizabeth Ann
> Said to her Nan
> 'Please will you tell me how God began.'

Remember that Nan's answer in the year 2100 would not be what it would now. But seriously, my good Sir, do you think that the human intellect, in its present stage of development, is capable of providing answers to such questions? If so, you are in fact asking a child, who has just learnt draughts, to adjudicate the end-game of two world masters in chess. He understands that an extraordinarily intricate game is in process. But he cannot grasp it because he does not know all the moves, though he may some day. Which, with the questions you ask, I don't think Man will, because he will never learn all the moves.

Q. In view of what he's done in a few centuries, I'd have thought he well might learn them, in a few million years. Human progress seems to be at a geometrical rate.

I. We obviously don't understand the same thing by 'progress', though I can't go into all that now. Simply this: unless that of Homo Sapiens quickly becomes less lop-sided, his expectation of life isn't going to be anything like your 'several million years'.

Q. Why not?

I. You seem to be leaving out of account altogether the present hideous discrepancy between the growth of Man's technological expertise, and that of his moral nature. Unless that is put right, it will destroy him. The more crack-brained theologians talk of Humanity having 'come of age'; when the real picture is that of a Humanity barely adolescent—at least that part of it which has political control—playing in a power-house of inconceivable force; and quite likely to press the thermo-nuclear button. Or, if it avoids that, to achieve some other, equally fatal, lunacy.

Q. But I thought you were a Christian, who prayed for the coming of God's kingdom upon earth; and also that you believed in Cosmic Process. Wouldn't either of them prevent such a lunacy?

I. The Kingdom of God will only come on earth if it comes in the hearts of men. That means, among other things, loving your neighbour as yourself, repaying no man evil for evil and forgiving your brother seventy times seven. As for Cosmic Process, Homo Sapiens would not be the first terrestrial species to become extinct. . . . But if, in destroying himself, Homo Sapiens at the same time biologically sterilizes this planet, I have no doubt at all that Cosmic Process will produce, elsewhere in the Universe—has, indeed, doubtless already produced—other beings more worthy of it.

Q. At least, if Humanity avoids the thermo-nuclear one, and the 'biological warfare' one, you and I won't be here to see the final lunacy.

I. No. And that is a timely reminder to a man in his seventh decade that your first question has still to be answered. You asked me what difference the conception of Cosmic Process makes to me personally. Here is my answer:

Before he was crucified, Christ told his disciples not to let their hearts be troubled. 'In my Father's house are many mansions. If it were not so, I would have told you. I go to prepare a place for you.' For me, the conception of Cosmic Process has brought a realisation, which I can find no language to express, of how many, how wonderful and how beautiful those mansions may reveal themselves to be.

BIBLIOGRAPHY

The following works, quoted or referred to, were published in this century. All others will be found in the Index.

Alexander, Samuel: *Space, Time and Deity* (1916).
Batho, Edith C.: *The Later Wordsworth* (1936).
Barthélemy-Madaule, M.: *Bergson et Teilhard de Chardin* (1963).
Beach, J. W.: *The Concept of Nature in 19th century English Poetry* (1936).
Bergson, Henri: *L'Evolution créatrice* (1907).
Bonhoeffer, Dietrich: *Letters and Papers from Prison* (1963).
Bradley, A. C.: *A Commentary on Tennyson's 'In Memoriam'* (1901).
—— *A Miscellany* (1929).
Bultmann, Rudolf: *Kerygma and Myth* (1953).
Chardin, P. Teilhard de: *Le Phénomène humain* (1955).
—— *Le Milieu divin* (1957).
—— *Science and Christ* (1965).
Clark, R. W.: *The Huxleys* (1968).
European Inheritance, The: 1954: (ed. Ernest Barker and others).
God I want, The: ed. James Mitchell (1967).
Gosse, Edmund: *Life of Swinburne* (1917).
Huxley, Julian: *Religion without Revelation* (1928).
—— *The Uniqueness of Man* (1841).
—— *Man in the Modern World* (1947).
—— *Evolution in Action* (1951).
—— *New Bottles for New Wine* (1957).
—— *Essays of a Humanist* (1964).
Jeans, James: *The Mysterious Universe* (1930).
King, Alec: *Wordsworth and the Artist's Vision* (1966).
Lovell, Bernard: *The Individual and the Universe* (1958).
Morgan, Conwy Lloyd: *Emergent Evolution* (1923).
—— *Life, Mind and Spirit* (1926).
Rader, Melvin: *Wordsworth, a Philosophical Approach* (1967).
Robinson, John: *Honest to God* (1963).
—— *Exploration into God* (1967).
Roppen, G.: *Evolution and Poetic Belief* (1956).
Russell, Bertrand: *History of Western Philosophy* (1946).

Rutland, William R.: *Swinburne, a 19th Century Hellene* (1931).
—— *Thomas Hardy, a Study of His Writings and their Background* (1938).
Swinburne, A. C.: *Letters*, ed. Cecil Y. Lang, 6 vols. (1959–62).
Tillich, Paul: *The Shaking of the Foundations* (1949).
—— *Systematic Theology*, 3 vols. (1957–64).
Tillyard, E. M. W.: *Five Poems* (1948).
Whitehead, A. N.: *Process and Reality* (1926).
Willey, Basil: *The 17th Century Background* (1938).
—— *19th Century Studies* (1949).

INDEX

Items followed by 'f.' continue on the following page(s). Notes are not indexed separately.

Alexander, Samuel 115
Arnold, Matthew 30
Baer, K. E. von 39
Balfour, A. J. 110
Barth, Karl 75
Bergson 92, 112
Bishop, Miss Bernadine 80, 82
Bonhoeffer, Dietrich 77
Booker, C 76
Bradley, A. C. 30 (and ch. 2 *passim*)
Bridgewater Treatises 28
Browning, Robert 29
Bruno, Giordano 8
Bultmann, Rudolph 78
Carducci 66
Carlyle 11, 55f.
Chardin, Teilhard de, ch. 4 *passim*
— Biography 91f.
— *Phenomenon of Man* (English version) 92f., 97
— Terminology 94f.
Comte 57f.
Copernicus 1
Cuvier 34
Dante 65, 66
Darwin, Charles 29, 31, 38
Descartes 83
Exploration into God 83f.
Galileo 1f.
Glanville, Joseph 9
God I want, The 80f.
Goethe 3, 9f., 20f., 27
— Eins und Alles 22
— Faust 9f., 23
— Metamorphosen der Tiere 21
— Natur Fragment, comment on 25
— Proaemion 26
— Weltseele 22, 24
Gosse, Sir Edmund 66, 67f.
Haeckel 45, 111
Haldane, J. B. S. 96
Hardy, Thomas 52, 116
Herschel 28
Honest to God 75f.
Huxley, Sir Julian 74, 85f., 93, 97, 101
— *Essays of a Humanist* 85

— Humanist Frame, The 87
— New Divinity, The 81, 89
— *Uniqueness of Man, The* 87
Huxley, Thomas Henry 86
Jeans, Sir James 59
King, Alec 15
Lamarck 24, 38
Laplace 24, 80
Lewis, C. S. 114
Linnaeus 34
Lodge, Sir Oliver 30
Lovell, Sir Bernard 59
Lyell 39
Mazzini 63f.
More, Henry 9
Mornet, Daniel 6
Newton, Sir Isaac 27
Nostradamus 10
Paracelsus 8
Pico della Mirandola 9
Platonists, Cambridge 9
Plotinus 8, 9
Powell, George 64, 69
Rader, M. 15, 18
Ragnarok 70
Robinson, Bishop John 75f.
Rousseau 6f.
Russell, Bertrand 21
Schelling 12f.
Selincourt, E. de 15, 18
Serres, A. E. R. 39
Shelley 35, 36, 70
Smuts, Jan 115
Spinoza 2f.
Swinburne 65f.
— Erechtheus 73
— Hertha 62, 68f.
— Hymn of Man 61, 66
— Mater Triumphalis 62
— Quia Multum Amavit 62
— Tiresias 64
Tennyson ch. 2, *passim*
— Ancient Sage, The 51
— Agryll, Lines to the Duke of 44
— De Profundis 44
— Higher Pantheism, The 43

— In Memoriam   ch. 2, *passim*
— Locksley Hall   34
— Maud   47
— Ode to the Duke of Wellington   53
— Palace of Art   32, 44
— Princess, The   32
— Timbuctoo   32
— Two Voices, The   50
Tiedemann, F.   39
Tillich, Paul   77f., 84
Tillyard, E. M. W.   68f.

Tobler, Georg Christoph   13
Ussher, James   94
Vestiges of Creation   37, 40f.
Whewell   28f.
Williams, H. A.   81, 82
Willey, Basil   59
Wordsworth   15f.
— Lines in early Spring   4
— Prelude   16f.
— Tintern Abbey   5, 7, 18
Yggdrasil   69f.